Garden Voices

Stories of Women and Their Gardens

Carolyn Freas Rapp

D1016700

⊞ Willow Creek Press

© 2007 Carolyn Freas Rrapp

Published by Willow Creek Press
P.O. Box 147, Minocqua, Wisconsin 54548

Printed in the United States

Cover and interior design: SQN Communications Design
Cover photograph: Sarah Hodzic-Fiorito
Cover image handtinting: Cherie Lester

Library of Congress Cataloging-in-Publication Data:

Rapp, Carolyn Freas.
  Garden voices : stories of women and their gardens /
Carolyn Freas Rapp.
    p. cm.
  Originally published: McLean, VA : Water Dance Press, c2005.
  ISBN 1-59543-590-5 (pbk.)
  1. Gardens—United States—Anecdotes. 2. Gardening—United
    States—Anecdotes. 3. Women gardeners—United States—
    Anecdotes. I. Title.
SB455.R33 2007
635.082'0973—dc22
                                              2006038713

To my mother, Florence Roberts Freas,
who encouraged me in all things,
and my father, Oscar Freas,
who taught me to see the beautiful world around me.

ACKNOWLEDGEMENTS

My heartfelt thanks go to all of the gardeners I interviewed for sharing so generously with me, especially to those whose conversations with me are the basis for this collection of stories.

To all whose steady encouragement resulted in the birth of this book into the world, I am deeply grateful. To my daughter Julie for her gentle but persistent status inquiries. To Sue Hodzic for her vision. To Nancy Kamens for her gift of listening. To Carol Freas for her perfectly-timed phone calls. To the women in my Dream Group who dreamed this book into being with me.

My gratitude goes to many others who helped me along the way:

To Martha Rapp, Mary MacBain, Judy Funderburk, and Meliss Bunce for reading the manuscript with so much care and love.

To Jenny Kavanaugh, Jim Rapp, Judy Robbins, Sarah Hodzic-Fiorito, Leslie Rollins, Nancy Kavanaugh, and Sam Robbins for having the skills to help me and the gift of appearing at just the right moment.

To my husband Michael, who helped me through the maze of computer technology and cheered me on.

Finally, a very special thank you goes to the two truly great gardeners in my life: Maria Chau, whose generosity in teaching and sharing the fruits of the garden is boundless; and Judy Funderburk, whose patience with the earth and ability to see the tiniest miracle never cease to amaze me and enrich my life.

CONTENTS

Introduction

Gardens have a way of bringing people together, like dogs and babies do. People discover they have something in common that they love and the conversations begin to flow. "You have a garden? So do I! What do you grow?" But the question that intrigues me most is "Why do you garden?" What got you started? What do you love so much about your garden that you're willing to spend countless hours on your knees in the hot sun?

I remember vividly when my own love affair with gardening began. It was the year that my first child was a senior in high school. The more he filled out college applications and prepared to leave home, the more I was seized by a deep and compelling urge to dig in the earth and grow things. Call it a reaction to impending loss. Chalk it up to having more free time. Blame it on hormones. Whatever it was that propelled me into the garden 12 years ago opened the door to a whole new world that continues to bring rich and unexpected treasures into my life.

From the day I proudly handed my mother her first bouquet of dandelions, I have been a flower lover. For most of my life I've dreamed of having a flower garden—preferably one of those luscious English country gardens that stop me in my tracks with longing as I page through garden magazines. But always the garden had been relegated to my "Someday…" file. As a working mother, I had an excuse. "I'm growing children," I would say. "I don't have time to grow anything else."

Now my world was shifting, and it was clear to me that my annual attempts at yard beautification—a dozen bedding plants here, a couple of azaleas there—would no longer satisfy. The earth was pulling me irresistibly toward something grand, inviting me to observe closely the miracle of minuscule seeds transforming into rows of leafy green lettuce, challenging me to be as reliable in raising its offspring as I was in raising my own children. I accepted the challenge willingly and the gifts I've received in return have come not only through my growing intimacy with the seasons and cycles of the earth, but also through my new common ground with gardeners, women gardeners in particular.

The first gift was my garden partner, Judy. For years she and I had met for bi-weekly breakfasts, hiked and biked together, swapped books, and poured out our hearts to each other. Why not garden together? The idea delighted her and within weeks we became the caretakers of a 20 x 30-foot plot in a lovely and lively community garden that we share to this day with 19 others.

The moment I first knelt down and began to turn the soil of our plot, I knew unmistakably that this was the right time of my life to be in a garden. The rich smell of the earth and the feel of my hands in the dirt awakened in me a world full of possibility, much like I had experienced in my early childhood spent mostly in a squat position with my face just inches from the ground in our back yard. It was the perfect antidote to the chapter of my life that was closing.

That whole sunny spring, I drove straight to the garden in every spare moment I could find—and I manufactured time I didn't have to slip in extra visits. I drank in the garden shops and nurseries in the area, intoxicated by the endless choices of all that I might put into and coax out of the earth. I persuaded my reluctant younger son and daughter to come help me plant, so eager was I to share my new love with them. As the seeds turned into peppers and tomatoes and zinnias, I took friends and family down to "meet" my garden, introducing it to them with the same pride I'd had when bringing my husband-to-be home to meet my parents.

At the same time, the other gardeners became a new family to me. I quickly learned that gardeners are among the most generous folks on earth and gratefully accepted their gifts, ranging from tomato plants in the spring to bunches of flowers and bags of beans in the summer to autumn seeds harvested from their crops. I was in awe of their knowledge, too. No matter what question I had—and as a novice I had many—there was someone within calling distance who knew the answer and was eager to help. Questions turned into conversations and conversations into friendships. Eventually, I became bold enough to begin asking some of the other women what their gardens meant to them.

The answers were often surprising. Michiko, a professional photographer whose specialty is photographing vegetables, began growing unusual vegetables when another photographer "stole" her unique photographic style. "Someone might be able to go to the grocery store and copy my strawberries and bananas," Michiko said, "but probably not my fava beans and bitter melons." Never could I have guessed that Michiko's garden is not only about vegetables, but also about creative integrity. Nor would I have discovered the rich world of Michiko's artistic life had I not dug beneath the mulch of everyday pleasantries.

Each woman had her own reason for gardening and that reason was intimately tied to her life—in every case, a very interesting life. I noticed, too, that gardening was not just something these women did. It was something with which each was in relationship, and they sometimes found that hard to express in words. My conversations with women in the community garden were so intriguing that I decided to venture beyond its fence and actually interview other women about their gardens.

Collecting these stories was like going on a treasure hunt, one that spanned years and moved at its own pace. I would interview a woman and she would say, "You should talk to my friend" or "I know someone who has a garden you should see." One garden led me to the next; each amazing woman pointed me toward another.

Every one of the women I spoke with feels that her garden is her intimate connection with the earth, the sacred Earth. For some, it is also a connection with other people and a place to make new friends, through a garden club or farmer's market or community garden. For others, the garden is a connection to the past, as they remember gardening with their mother, father, grandmother or grandfather. Still others prefer to be alone in their gardens and enjoy a moment of solitude. Whether she gardens alone or with someone else, every woman considers the garden a welcome and necessary escape from the fast-paced, high-tech world in which we live. It is simple, basic, and manageable.

For some women, the garden is a place of healing—healing from cancer for Susan and healing from grief for Beth. Gardens are magic, a place to commune with the world of nature spirits. They can also be a thread that connects to God or to the Higher Self. For many, the garden is a teacher and the most frequently-learned lesson is patience—and its often-unexpected rewards. Some women wear gloves. Others love dirt under their fingernails. Some find weeding therapeutic; some hate it. And still others are philosophical about weeds. "A weed is just a plant out of place," says Carol, an artist. "Weeds are quite lovely if you look at them closely. What I've learned in my garden has enriched my life, because now I have friendships with people whom I might otherwise have passed over as 'weeds'."

I feel honored to have had the opportunity to meet each of these gardeners. Most of the gardens I visited would not find their way onto the glossy pages of gardening magazines, but that isn't the motivation for these women. They build their worlds around their gardens because it satisfies their need to create and it fills their souls. By taking me into their gardens, they allowed me a glimpse of their deepest selves.

I invite you now to meet these wise, funny, energetic, creative, spirit-filled, independent, courageous, nurturing, hard-working, earth-connected women. First, I'll introduce each one to you. Then she will take you into her garden and into her world.

If you are a beginning gardener or thinking about getting started, I hope that these stories will plunge you wholeheartedly into gardening. If you are a longtime or master gardener, perhaps these stories will add another layer to the richness of your own story in the garden.

As for me, I consider it good fortune that I postponed having a garden for so long. When you discover a passion later in life there is a better chance that it will take you all the way to the end. I know that I will garden for as long as I am able. And now that I've learned that the climate I live in is too hot and too fraught with tempestuous thunderstorms to be hospitable to the English garden of my dreams, I can take that project off of my "Someday…" list. But that's all right. The garden I have is the perfect garden for me. It is moderately lovely, highly productive, and it comes with a partner and a loving garden family. Best of all, it inspired this collection of stories that will last long after I've picked my last zinnia and harvested my last tomato.

Susan's Garden

A Circle of Stones

Susan

Susan loves experiments. When I arrived to have lunch and talk about her garden, the vegetable casserole in the oven was an experiment. It turned out to be a great success, which was lucky for me. Susan says that when she tries a new concoction for a guest she doesn't know well, a good outcome is a sign that they'll be friends. If the food turns out badly, she has to rethink the possibilities for friendship.

Like her casserole, Susan's house is an experiment that combines old with new and beautiful art with reclaimed discards. There are stunning bowls and pots and baskets that she has collected at art shows. An old wooden chicken hatchery serves as a coffee table, a bread cabinet is her end table, and each dining room chair is different. Susan is an artist by nature, if not by profession, so her house continually changes, much like an artist paints over and adds to the canvas. "It's not the destination that's important," she says. "It's the process, what happens on the way."

So it is with her garden. Susan has only been working on it for several years, fitting it in around a demanding full-time job in human resource development, but her garden is steadily expanding. When she began our garden tour, I thought of a greeting card I once saw that said, "Come into my garden. I'd like my plants to meet you." She knows every petunia and every geranium personally. They are friends that she has chosen carefully and checks on often. She introduced each plant by name and told me a story about when it came to live with her, how it has adapted, how it is withstanding slug and mite attacks, and what its prognosis is.

Susan's life changed dramatically several years ago, when she was diagnosed with cancer. Those who knew her were inspired by her courage and learned a lot from her about the healing power of laughter. Now, as I walk through the garden with her, it is hard to imagine that the prognosis for her life is anything but long and filled with endless, fascinating experiments.

Susan's Garden

A CIRCLE OF STONES

I was sitting at my desk at work when I got the call. My doctor tried to tell me as gently as she could, but it was still brutal. "It's not good, Susan," she said. "You do have cancer." I didn't say anything. "Susan," she asked, "are you all right?" I said, "Yes, I'm just trying to think what we do next." "Good," she said. "I knew you'd take that attitude."

She explained the options. I wanted the treatment to be as minimal as possible, so I chose to have a lumpectomy and we scheduled a time for the operation. Then I went into the ladies room and cried. When I came out, I called everyone in the office together because I don't believe in keeping things secret. I said, "I want you all to know that I do have cancer and I have to have surgery. So we need to sit down and talk about how we're going to get things done while I'm gone." I teared up and everyone else teared up. "Enough of that!" I said. "Let's get going and decide how to handle this." I really think it helps to take action.

I had the operation in February. My children are grown and they were wonderful, but if I hadn't had family, I wouldn't have felt alone because people came out of the woodwork to help me.

I had to wait three weeks before I started radiation and then I had 33 treatments, which began in March. Coming back from the first day of radiation, I decided to take a back road instead of the highway because I wanted to stop by the dog pound. I always said I would get a dog when I retired, but now I had cancer and I wasn't waiting another day. On the way to the pound, I saw a stone-yard. I've always loved stones, so I pulled over and went in. As I stood there looking at all the beautiful stones, the idea came to me: "I'm going to build a path." That day I bought three stones.

Now, I wasn't supposed to be lifting anything at all. So I was careful to choose flagstones that weren't too heavy. The other prerequisite was that they had to be irregular in shape. I don't like things that are regular. I don't like two's and four's—I think three's and five's and seven's are much more interesting. Maybe that comes from when I was a weaver. There's much more excitement in a three-stripe or five-stripe scarf, as opposed to two or four stripes.

When I told the doctor what I was doing she said, "You're buying stones? How big?" I said, "I can lift them." She paused, then asked, "Are they making you happy?" "Yes," I said, "I'm building a path." "All right," she finally agreed. "But not too heavy."

I put the first stone at the entrance to my back yard, at the bottom of the hill. I have steps there now, but there weren't any steps then, just a jungle of weeds. After my husband and I divorced fifteen years ago, I completely abandoned the garden and the yard, except to have the grass mowed. Actually, I stopped gardening while I was married. I had expected that the garden would be something my husband and I would do together, like my mother and father did. But he had no interest, and not having someone to share the garden with spoiled it for me. So I just stopped—until the first day of my radiation treatments when I put down the first flagstone.

I bought one or two or three stones each time I stopped at the stoneyard on the way back from radiation, depending on how much money I had in my pocket that day. I wasn't very hungry during those months, so most of my food budget was going into rocks!

After the first stone, the path just built itself. I'd look at the last stone I had laid and say, "What fills this notch here?" Then I'd put the next stone down. And so on. I did it the way I do my art, where I'm not conscious of anything but the flow of the process. I ended up with a circle, which is a symbol of eternity, but I didn't plan that. It just happened.

Day after day, I brought home rocks and the actual placing of them became a ritual for me. There was also something important about the lifting. It required strength and it was giving me purpose, as if in the act of lifting and placing the rocks I was saying, "I still have two hands to do things with, and even though it's painful, I'm moving forward." Actively doing something was much better than sitting inside feeling sorry for myself.

I think rocks are beautiful. I've broken a lot of fingernails and scraped my hands gathering rocks over the years. Rocks are solid and they have age, like old furniture. Most of the pieces of furniture in my house are old and I love imagining the people who might have used the chairs and the tables and the chests at one time or another. Good experience, bad experience, it's all built in, and there's strength in that. Stones have history built into them, too. Stones have strength.

I started my treatments in March and finished in May, so as I was building the path, spring bloomed. All around me there was new growth and new life. At the same time, a friend began to help me with the garden. I didn't know Judy very well when we started, but when you work side by side with someone, things spill out and you get to know each other in a different way. Through building a friendship, the garden and its path took on a spiritual dimension for me.

Judy was extremely supportive. Sometimes I felt terribly guilty because I didn't have the strength to do the heavy work. But she didn't complain. "You need this done? Let's do it!" she'd say. So I'd do a little digging and she'd do a lot of digging. I'd do a little pruning and she'd do a lot of pruning. She also brought me pots and pots of plants. Yet I've always felt that I made the choices about my garden. I knew what I wanted the garden to look like and Judy helped me get the right plants. That sharing was so special, probably because of the memories I have of my mother and father sharing their garden. I remember summer mornings when my father would go out to the garden, bring my mother a rose, and lay it on her pillow so that she would wake up to its sweet scent. Sometimes he would say to me, "C'mon, Susan, we're going to go get Mom a rose." Then Dad and I would go out to the garden and pick the rose together.

The day I had my last radiation treatment was the day I bought the last stone for the path. After that, I didn't have time to go out of my way to the stoneyard. But I've continued to work on the garden and it just keeps getting prettier all the time. I have more than 70 different varieties of plants and flowers and at least 500 plants. Part of the garden is in the shade, and that's most gorgeous in April and May when Jacob's ladder, columbine, Jack-in-the-pulpit and lots of other spring flowers burst up out of the ground. In the summer, the daylilies and black-eyed Susans and coneflowers are a mass of color, and once I counted 17 butterflies on my butterfly bush. Then, of course, it's so much fun to prepare food in the summer with all the basil and thyme and dill and tarragon I grow.

When I got a clean bill of health at the end of the treatments, I threw a party to celebrate and to thank all the friends who were so supportive. I called it my "Radiation Celebration" and, wouldn't you know, they brought me things. Here I was trying to thank them and they brought me gifts. A beautiful hydrangea. A peony tree. An astilbe. All of them are flourishing and when I walk or work in my garden, I feel as if my friends are there with me.

People say that cancer is a wake-up call. And it is. You realize that you don't have time to waste, and I realized that I could not continue to do the job I had. I was operations manager for a consulting firm, so I had to use my logical left brain when I'm really a right-brain person, an artist. After the cancer, I went to my boss and said, "I can't do this job anymore. I don't know how we can change things, but I can't do it any longer." So we sat down, all the support staff in the office, and looked at the job responsibilities. We went through our skills and we changed positions. The technology person is now the operations manager, and I moved into a role that includes both graphics and human resources, jobs that are much more suited to me. I don't know whether I would have been able to do this in another firm, but when my company was willing to make changes to keep me with it, I felt immensely valued. Of course, it took cancer to make me speak up and claim what my heart really wanted.

I made other changes, too. I got my dog. I had a deck built so that I could sit and look out at the garden. And I started taking the art classes that I had put off for so long. I began my first class at the end of March, less than halfway through my radiation treatments. It was a silkscreen class and I was so stiff that I had to have the teacher help me move the paint across the screen. But it felt so right. Then I just started taking class after class. Collage, monotype, watercolor, and I really got into papermaking. I took eleven classes in one year.

The more art there was in my life, the more my garden grew, and I think that's because every creative act feeds every other creative act. I used to think I had to have a career in art to be happy, but I know now that I don't. I just have to live a creative life.

Recently, I began to build a path off to the right of the original circle path. I'm using some of the paving stones my father gave me. My father loved stones, too. He had an accounting business and did quite a bit of traveling in New Jersey in the 1950s when they were tearing up cobblestone streets and replacing them with hardtop. He'd come home from a trip with his trunk full of cobblestones—just like I came home from the stoneyard with my trunk full of flagstones! Last year, my parents moved out of the house they had lived in for 50 years and I brought the last of Dad's cobblestones home with me. I also brought three plants from their garden that are very special to me because they are all that's left of home. A tiger lily. A lily-of-the-valley. And a beautiful, hardy plant with pink flowers that my mother always called a "live-forever."

Sue's Garden

Peace and Celebration

Sue

When Sue was 19, she came to the United States from England, where she was trained as a hair stylist. She brought not only skills, but also charm and a delightful British accent. Fifteen years ago, I was looking for a hairdresser. One of my friends said, "Go to Sue. She only takes one client at a time, she plays soothing music, her shop is lovely, and her garden could be in *Better Homes and Gardens*." Trouble was, she had a waiting list months long. I decided to put my name on it, and when my turn finally came, I knew I had made the right decision the moment I stepped into her beautiful garden.

Sue says that her goal is to create a sense of peace in her garden. She wants people to walk into it and leave the worries of their lives at the front steps. She wants them to feel transformed by its beauty. And she has succeeded. As her client for many years, that's exactly what I experience each time I walk in and out of her shop.

But her clients aren't the only ones who feel something special when they walk into her garden. The day I interviewed her, we were sitting on the back deck overlooking her garden when the service man from the gas company arrived to check on a suspected gas leak. As he walked through the yard to the kitchen door, he passed beneath the arbor, then just stopped and stared out at the garden. "Did you do all this?" he asked incredulously. Sue nodded. He stared a moment longer, then turned to her and said, "Ma'am, I think I've just walked into the Garden of Eden." In a way he had—a garden so lovely that it provided a glimpse of heaven.

Sue's Garden

PEACE AND CELEBRATION

More than anything else, my garden has been a place of peace for me. I was born toward the end of World War II in Liverpool, England, which was very badly bombed during the war. My father was a pilot in the Royal Air Force and ten days after my birth, his plane was shot down over Germany and he was killed. I carry the trauma of that beginning in my body and my search has always been for peace.

The first time I experienced the peace a garden can bring was as a very little girl in my grandfather's garden. The story goes that when my family couldn't find me, my sister would say, "Well, you know where Sue is. She's playing with the fairies at the bottom of the garden." And she was right. My grandfather had a wonderful garden with a winding path through trellised roses that led to neatly planted rows of lettuce, carrots, potatoes, and tomatoes. Then farther down, he had a greenhouse with year-round chrysanthemums, a grapevine, and tomatoes. All I have to do is close my eyes and I can smell it to this day. At the very bottom of the garden, there were huge rhubarb plants, with leaves so big I could hide under them, and that's where I found the fairies and played with them. It was a magical place where even as a little girl I experienced safety and peace.

So when I came to America, my dream was to have a home with a beautiful garden, and that's what I've created here. Not only for myself, but so that others, too, can experience the magic of a garden and the peace it can bring.

The path into my hairdressing shop curves around the house and through the gardens. People walk through an arbor, as if entering another world. There's a bench so that they can sit down and enjoy the garden before or after an appointment. My wish is that when they leave my shop, they will not only be more beautiful on the outside, but more peaceful on the inside.

Every single day of the year that it is humanly possible, I begin my day in the garden. The first warm morning in February, I'm out on the deck with my coat and scarf, trying to grab enough sun to have my coffee outside. Having to spend so much time inside during the winter is quite hard for me. It's remarkable how different I feel when I can sit outside—and quite noticeable what a difference my garden makes to my sense of well-being.

Truth be told, I'd rather sit and look at my garden than work in it. But all the work is worthwhile for the peace and joy it brings me. My garden is a visual tool that helps me move into the quiet, still place within myself, the place that I call the Higher Self or the God Self. It is a place of deep meditation, and sitting quietly and absorbing the beauty helps me remember to connect to the spiritual aspect of myself. There are days when my mind is so cluttered with the daily concerns and anxieties of life that I come to my garden barely able to see the beauty all around me. But as I sit and slowly shift into the still, peaceful place that I have come to learn is within me, my garden literally begins to sparkle and I feel better able to deal with whatever the day may bring.

What I've really done is create sacred space in my yard—a garden that enables me to move into the spiritual realms of my life. I love to sit by the little fountain because of the sound of the burbling water and because that's where I can smell the lavender. In the afternoon, the birds come to the birdbath and put on quite a show, primping and cleaning themselves up! The butterfly bush is always full of brilliant, fluttering wings and the hummingbirds flock to the sugar water in the feeder. It is so easy for me to find peace in my garden and to experience the divine through nature.

My garden is also about family and celebration. Both of my children were born in May and every single birthday party has been on the lawn. Each year we put up the badminton net and the croquet set. We've dunked for apples, played water balloon games, and had clowns entertain us. We've had an engagement party, anniversary parties, and even a wedding—all surrounded by the beauty of my flowers. What joy my garden has given me through celebrations that have brought family and friends together!

One year my daughter and I started a new ritual, a mother-daughter garden day. We worked together in the garden, planted many beautiful flowers, took photos of them, and kept a journal of our thoughts and experiences together in the garden. This has been a great gift for both of us.

Creating rituals has been an important part of my garden experience, so I should not have been surprised at what happened several years ago when my sister and I decided to make a pilgrimage to my father's grave in Germany. Our mother had planned to take us there one day, but never did. Sadly, she had a stroke and died when she was only 49, twenty years to the day after my father died.

When I met my sister in London, we decided to go first to my mother's cemetery. My mother loved roses and each time we moved during my childhood, the first thing she did at the new house was to plant a rose garden. As she had requested, we sprinkled her ashes on a rose garden in a cemetery in Liverpool. When we arrived, we sat quietly by the rose garden and it came to us to take some of the soil from that garden with us to Germany. We also bought two small English rose bushes. Then we set off for the cemetery in Bavaria, where my father was buried along with hundreds of other brave soldiers.

We approached the cemetery by walking down a quiet, beautifully manicured country road. It was wonderful to see how diligently this cemetery was being taken care of. We found our father's grave, and for the first time in my life I got a real sense of him. There was something enormously powerful about standing in front of his grave, reading his name, seeing his birth date and the date his airplane was shot down, reading the names of the seven other men who were in the plane with him, and seeing them all there together.

We knelt and cried. Then we took the soil and the rose bushes and planted them, one on each side of his tombstone. The experience was deeply moving for us. It felt as if we were connecting our mother and father to each other, and the tiny rose bushes were all four of us coming together, connecting us as the family we had never known. My life was changed that day through the power of the soil, the plants, and the ritual. A peace came over me—the peace I had been seeking in the garden since I was a little girl.

I wanted to bring that peace back with me to my own garden,

so I took a small clipping from a plant that was growing beside my father's grave. I didn't know if it would survive the long trip home, but it did. I planted it in the center of my garden and it has doubled in size and wintered over several years. It gets pretty yellow flowers on it in the spring and reminds me always of how life goes on, with its beauty and its sorrow. It reminds me of the peace I can find in my garden.

Joan's Garden

To Market, To Market

Joan

Early morning at the local farmer's market is one of the most delicious moments of my week. Immersed in the vibrant color and aroma of fruits and vegetables and herbs, and carried along by the gentle rhythm of people strolling, squeezing, choosing, and chatting with the sellers, it is easy for me to forget for a moment the long "To Do" list that will shape the rest of my day. Life at the farmer's market is slow and easy.

For me, that is. For Joan and the other farmers who show up at the market week after week, it is anything but easy. Joan picks her crops the day and evening before market and prepares them for transport. She gets up at 4 a.m.—on the days she "sleeps in"—and drives an hour and a half into town from Featherbed Farm out in the Virginia countryside. She has to contend with too much rain or too little, too much sun or not enough, bugs that eat her crops, and vermin that steal them. But she farms anyway and when she pulls her truck into market and sets out her crisp leaf lettuce, perfect haricots verts, blueberries, basil, peppers, squash, and ripe, red tomatoes, I am grateful. So are other people. That's why we all stand in line and put our names on waiting lists for her food.

I drove out to Featherbed Farm on a golden September day with not a single cloud in the blue sky. The swaying branches of an ancient weeping willow ushered me up Joan's dirt driveway. On the left was a large, red barn, and on the right her restored 1760 home and the greenhouse where the cycle of a new growing season begins each February. Parked beside the barn was the big, green pickup truck that goes to market on weekends with its license plate,

"VA GROWN." Joan and I talked for a while in the house, then she took me on a tour of her garden. The sun was warm, the breeze was soft, and I never wanted to leave to go back to the city. But then, I'm not the one who works to keep this whole big operation going. Joan is.

Joan's Garden

TO MARKET, TO MARKET

It is very exciting to me to grow food that feeds people. My family needs shelter, they need clothing, they need food. To know that all by myself I can take care of one third of my family's requirements—that we could literally live on what I can grow—gives me a great feeling of satisfaction. And to have people buy the food I grow, besides being fun, is rewarding because they get sustenance from it. Plus I have to admit I like the ego boost of having people say, "Those are the best blueberries I've ever tasted."

I did not move out into the country in order to have a garden. We bought this land because it was affordable and it was not in the city. My husband was born and raised in New York City and I grew up in the suburbs of Washington, D.C. Neither of us had any real concept of what country life was like. But after ten years of working in the nation's capital, we had both had enough. It was an angry city at the time, with crime and drugs and all kinds of things that were just not a part of the way we wanted to spend our lives.

So there we were in 1974, the new owners of 23 acres in the country. When I looked out over all that land, the obvious thing to do was to plant a garden. So I did, and that's how it all started. My husband still commutes into the city, but I quit my job after a year because it was clear to me that there was no way I could take care of this farm and build it back up if I continued to work in the city. Just cutting the grass is a job in itself. But I love being out here. The quiet and the solitude suit me well. In fact, I would describe myself as a hermit until I began to sell at the farmer's market.

I started my first garden with the everyday vegetables that everybody can grow successfully if they just put the seeds or the plants in the ground. Tomatoes, peppers, squash, corn. But I started big—with sixty tomato plants! I also started canning that summer. I created a summer kitchen in the springhouse where I had a propane stove and a gas refrigerator. We have no central air conditioning and it would have made our house unbearable in the summer heat and humidity to have those boiling cauldrons in our kitchen. I made ketchup and pickles and put up countless quarts of tomatoes.

When the children were born in 1979 and 1981, the garden shrank to about a dozen tomato plants and just enough of the other vegetables to pick for meals. When the children were infants, I bought two CB radios. I put one in their room and took the other one out to the garden with me so I could hear them if they cried. It was my version of a child-monitoring system because I just couldn't bear to sit in the house while they were napping. There was way too much to do outside, and even though I didn't actually have to grow our food like women often did in the past, I needed to do this for my mental health.

When the children got older, they came out to the garden with me. But neither of them ever got interested in gardening, probably because they saw the amount of time and involvement it required.

I never encouraged them, either. Gardening has always been my thing and maybe I worked subconsciously to keep it that way, so that it would remain my refuge, my personal space. Daniel has his drums. Heidi has her books and computer. My husband has his professional life. The garden is mine, one little corner all my own.

About 12 years ago, something happened that changed my way of thinking about growing food. There were some Mexicans— migrant workers—at a stable across the way. They would come over to my garden, pick up tomatoes that had fallen to the ground, and take them home to eat. Seeing this made me very sad. It was not right that people should have to take food off the ground, so I started growing more tomatoes to give to them. I also planted hot peppers, because I thought they would like them. And they did. They were grateful and friendly, and when they came over for the vegetables, we would have little conversations.

This experience introduced me to the idea that there might be a role for me to grow food for others beyond my family—that there is a bigger family to feed. That's how my garden started to expand. Two years later, the operation down the road changed and there were no more migrant workers. But my garden was still just as big—about half an acre and close to 300 tomato plants. Participating in the farmer's market seemed like a good way to sell some of the excess. That was ten years ago and it's been a full-time venture ever since.

I started by taking my food to two of the county farmer's markets. You have to apply and send in a statement signed by a county official certifying that you are growing everything yourself. From these applications they choose farmers who will offer a range of products at the market. Farmers are eligible to apply if they live within a 125-mile radius of the market. But farmer's markets have become so popular since the early 1990s that there are just not enough farmers to supply them all. Competition for farmers is so keen that some of the markets have had to shut down.

Right now, I'm doing three markets—on Friday, Saturday, and Sunday. What I take to market depends on the season. When the markets open up in the beginning of May, my main crop is lettuce. I get up around 1:30 in the morning and wear a miner's headlamp because lettuce has to be picked the same day you take it to market. I'm the only farmer who does this. Everyone else picks the day before, but I'm convinced those few hours make a difference.

In fact, there is a "best time" to pick nearly everything. I pick blueberries after the sun is off of them, in the evening or night, but before any dew settles. There are only a certain number of hours you can pick blueberries and have them be at their peak. Basil should be picked at night, not in the dark, but about 8 o'clock. You should pick parsley and cilantro in the morning. Thyme and the other woodier stemmed plants like oregano and rosemary can be picked at any time. So can tomatoes as long as they're not wet, and that's mainly to prevent disease from spreading. Squash are best picked in the morning. Heat tends to draw the water, which is why the leaves of squash plants are wilted in the hot sun. In the morning, both the plant and the squash itself will have more moisture in them, so the squash will be firmer and better. Peas and beans can be picked at any time.

Some days are very rushed. On the days when I get up at 1:30 in the morning, I often haven't gone to bed until midnight the night before, so basically I lie down for an hour. The blueberries I pick in the evening have to be packaged. I grow sprouts and they require quite a bit of work with packaging. I pack my tomatoes in sawdust so that they get to market without bruising. Obviously, if I picked all day long and piled my tomatoes into bushel baskets, I would take a lot more to market. Doing it my way limits the amount I can sell. It also stresses me out because I'm afraid I'm not going to get everything done before I have to leave for market. Then all the way there I have a knot in my stomach for fear that people will come and tell me that everything they bought last week was horrible. It's very hard for a hermit to go to market!

In the summer, when the lettuce crop is finished, I don't have to get up until four o'clock. But when I get back from the Saturday market, I have to start all over again for the Sunday market. So there's no time for a nap. I try to get to bed at a decent hour on Friday night, because I just can't go for 48 hours without any sleep. Not at my age!

I get a lot of gratifying comments, so that validates my way of doing things. And people even want to get onto lists to buy my food. For example, I grow those skinny little French green beans— haricots verts. They have to be picked every day twice a day so they don't get too big and I can spend hours picking them. I charge eight dollars a pound, yet I have a waiting list far longer than I can possibly supply of people who are willing to pay that for beans. Can you imagine? I suppose it's these customers, people who really do appreciate the difference in quality, that keep me doing it.

Then there's the weather to contend with. During most of the 90s, we had horrible summers. Either the spring was very, very late or very, very wet. Summers were hot and dry, except that a few years ago it rained the entire summer and everybody's crops had molds and diseases. I would hate to have to rely on farm marketing for an income. I have never had any kind of monetary goal because in farming, if you do, you're just setting yourself up for disappointment nine times out of ten. I have always seen the farmer's market as something that I could do to make my love of being outdoors legitimate. I do, however, like getting paid for what I'm doing because people are showing that they value my work by giving me what society equates with approval—namely, money.

I never take vacations. Never. From February until May when things are in the greenhouse, even going away one day from seven in the morning until seven at night is hard because things dry out too much. Then spring comes and the crops go in. Then the markets start. When the children were young, my husband took them on vacations and I stayed home.

People ask me how many more years I'm going to do this. Some days it seems like one more year is more than I can bear. Then other days I can't imagine not doing it. My husband wants me to retire so that we can travel together. I don't know. I don't know how far I'd get from home because I don't like to be away. I'm happiest right here.

I'm a weaver and a spinner and I might spend more time on that. It has mostly faded out of my life as I've gotten more into the market. But spinning and weaving are not so different from farming. You take something from its beginning—a seed or fleece from a sheep—and you carry it through to its final use, to something you eat or something you wear. Either way, there is a fundamental connection with the earth and I like being part of that.

Nancy's Garden

The Men I Love

Nancy

Many of the women I spoke with traced their love of gardening back to their childhood and a special man. While Mom or Grandmom was in the kitchen, the little girl was out in the back garden, digging in the dirt with Dad or Granddad. When Nancy talks about the years of gardening with her father, her voice becomes animated by happy memories and she laughs as she remembers how the garden transformed her serious father into a fun, funny playmate.

Now she gardens with her husband, which brings up the whole issue of men and women together in the garden. Some years ago I met a woman who was researching a book on relationships and she told me that of the couples she interviewed, the garden was often a metaphor for their marriage. Some couples work together harmoniously in the garden and the product is better because of each other's input. Others find that the magic of the garden is in creating beauty together. And still others use the garden as a tangible way to remind themselves of boundaries or "turf." Separate "his and her gardens" allow each partner the space to express an individual vision and remind them that they may need space in other realms of their relationship as well. Each married woman I interviewed mentioned the role (or non-role) of her husband. Nancy's experience centers around making a garden with a man and making it work.

There is also another man present when Nancy gardens—her son, David, who died 12 years ago of AIDS at the age of 21. Nancy moved through that difficult journey with courage and compassion, and she finds solace and healing in her garden. But for all the men in her story, it would not be complete without mentioning that she has passed her love of gardening on to her daughter. I called to talk with Nancy one beautiful spring Sunday and she said, "I can't. I'm going over to Heather's to help her put in her first garden at her new house. I'll call you back later."

Nancy's Garden

THE MEN I LOVE

Almost every memory I have of gardens is connected to the men I have loved: my grandfather, my father, my husband, and my son. I've spent many hours gardening with the first three, and I've spent many hours sitting in the memorial garden we created in our back yard for my son David after he died.

Both of my grandparents on my father's side were avid gardeners. They grew vegetables and flowers, and every garden they planted was beautiful. Beauty was especially important to my grandmother, and people would often stop to tell her how wonderful her roses were. Grammy and Grampy spent hours and hours together in the garden. Watching the enjoyment they got out of it, I came to believe as a child that the garden is a place where men and women come together to have fun and create.

When my mother married my father, she knew nothing about gardening, so my grandmother came over and helped her create her own beautiful gardens. I inherited my love of beauty from my grandmother and my mother, but it was my father I spent time with in the garden.

He planted vegetables—no flowers, just a huge vegetable garden. I think there is something very nurturing about a man who gardens. In my family, my mother was the main nurturer. On the other hand, my father had a lively, difficult personality and he was on the road a lot with his job. But he loved his garden and I think that he saw all those luscious vegetables and fruits he grew as his way of providing for and nurturing his family.

Of course, I didn't think about that at the time. I just thought the garden was fun. Big fun, because Dad's garden was more than an acre and we lived in a town, not on a farm. Dad grew so many strawberries that my sister and I set up a stand out in front of our house and sold strawberries just like other kids sold lemonade. There were still plenty left for us to have strawberries and cream in the morning and strawberry shortcake at night. That was back in the days when you couldn't get strawberries year-round in the grocery store, so we waited for strawberry season every year with great anticipation. It's hard to find strawberries that taste that sweet anymore. In fact, no strawberries have ever tasted as good as the ones from my father's garden.

He started out with the garden in our yard, then he cut down part of the woods behind our house to make another garden. For a special treat, he would attach a cart to the back of his little tractor and pull my sister and me all around the fields and through paths in the woods up to a little pond. The garden was where his playful side came out. As an adult, I can look back and see that my father was overwhelmed with the responsibility of providing for his family. He traveled a great deal and was often very tired. But in the garden I got to know a completely different person with a mischievous sense of humor.

He loved to play tricks. One day he brought a Coke bottle into the house with a big cucumber inside of it. "How did that cucumber get in there?" I asked him, totally amazed. "Magic," he whispered mysteriously. A couple of days later, he took me out to the garden with an empty bottle and showed me how you lay the bottle next to the cucumber plant, put a tiny cucumber in it, and let it grow until it fills the bottle. When my cucumber grew big, I showed the bottle to my friends and told them it was magic!

The one thing I didn't like about my father's garden was weeding it. My father fertilized the garden with cow manure and didn't put down straw or any other kind of ground cover, so there was always an enormous, healthy crop of weeds. It was my sister's and my job to pull them up. But we also got to pick crops with Dad. We'd yank those baby carrots up, wipe off the dirt, and eat them right there in the field. Tomatoes, too. Nothing is more delicious than food you pick and eat on the spot. I don't remember ever seeing my father happier than when he was in the garden.

My first husband had no interest in gardening. But I remember that on a trip I took to England with a group of Girl Scouts, we stayed in a small hotel that was owned by a couple. The woman took care of the hotel and the man took care of the lovely gardens that surrounded it. I thought, "Wow, isn't it wonderful to have a man who gets up in the morning and gardens before he goes to work." But at the time I didn't understand the connection between gardening and nurturing or why it was so special to me.

Some years after my divorce, I met Jerry. It was at a party in the fall and he came in jeans and a tee shirt because he had just finished putting in bulbs for his spring gardens. He was divorced, too, and had just moved into a new house. The first thing he did was plant a garden. That was all I needed to hear. We were married six weeks later!

I wish I could say that we gardened "happily ever after," but that's not the way it worked out. We are still happily married, but gardening has been an evolving process and we've had to work some things out. In fact, I think our gardens are a reflection of the evolution of our marriage.

When we got married, we moved into his house. We had five children between us, so the inside became my territory. The outside was his, which was fine with me because there were always beautiful flowers all around the house. In a way, Jerry was my own personal gardener. It was such a gift and I felt so cared for.

But eventually, when the children were a little older, I wanted to get outside and be part of the garden myself. That has been the tricky part—transforming it from "his" garden to "our" garden, because Jerry was very protective of that space. In the fall, he would choose all his bulbs and plant them for his spring gardens of tulips and narcissus. In the winter, he would go through all the catalogs to plan his summer gardens and buy his seeds. He loves to grow things from seeds, under lights, while my style of gardening is to go to the nursery, buy the plants, arrange them in a shape that pleases me, and create instant beauty. So gardening with Jerry was an adjustment for me. I had to slow down.

For Jerry, one of the challenges has been to reconsider the shapes of his gardens. Initially, the garden was just a square plot. I got very frustrated with it because I could envision lots of different shapes and curves that were much more interesting to me. But it was very hard for him to let go of his square. One night we sat down with a pencil and paper. I said, "How about this?" and drew a circle. He looked at it for a couple of minutes then he drew a square on top of the circle. After a little more reflection, he turned the paper and said, "If we just move it around like this, it makes a cone shape." That year we struggled and compromised and came up with a cone-shaped garden—partly square and partly round.

Another thing I persuaded Jerry to give up on was his vegetable garden. We have a lot of shade in the yard, but Jerry is a very persevering guy. Year after year he would put in rows of tomato plants and harvest six or eight tomatoes. He even tried a crop of corn. I think he finally listened to me because of all the years I spent in my father's vegetable garden that got full sun. We planted a shade garden where the vegetables had been.

As each season passed, there was more give and take. One year I suggested that we move the birdbath closer to the house in order to plant a bed of flowers in its place where there is more sun. Jerry was afraid the birdbath would be too close to the house and the birds wouldn't come. But they do, and now we have both birds and more flowers in the yard. Last year he saw a Japanese garden and came home with the idea of making one in our back yard. I couldn't envision it so I just said, "Go ahead." He put a wooden ornamental piece in the garden, which looked very nice. But then he put a lot of crushed white stone around it, which was too bright and garish. I said, "I'm sorry, but I just don't like the white stone." He was so unhappy that I was unhappy that we got down on our hands and knees and picked out all the white stones. We put mulch around it and it looks lovely.

Then there is David's garden at the bottom of the yard. Our son died in February 1992, and we were bereft. In the spring of that year, Jerry said, "I want to make a garden for David." He picked the place and we made the garden together. I've always loved little spaces, so Jerry put up a wall to make it private. We chose an arbor, a bench, and a statue, then we planted flowers. Jerry's hammock is there so he goes down to read. I like to sit on the bench and meditate, especially in the spring when the garden is enclosed by brilliant pink azaleas. We've even had a couple of rituals in David's garden. To mark his first birthday after his death, the family gathered and we had a little birthday party in the garden. It was much more comforting than sad. I'm keenly aware of David's presence in the garden.

The gardens in our yard really do reflect the journey of our lives. Recently, a neighbor dropped by who had moved away 12 years ago. She asked me if we still had our garden of impatiens in the back yard. It reminded me that we used to have impatiens that were so big they were like bushes. They're smaller now because in the past twelve years the tree canopy has grown so large that the yard is much more shaded. When we moved here 20 years ago, there was a lilac bush at the side of the yard, but with the increasing shade and the fence our neighbors built, it just didn't get enough light. Now the lilac bush is gone and we have hanging baskets of flowers on the fence. In the spring, little white roses cascade over from our neighbor's yard. Everything keeps changing in the garden.

As for Jerry and me, we've changed, too. Our garden is pretty much a collaboration now and our relationship is more harmonious and more integrated than it has ever been. The sections of his life that I didn't know about and boundaries that even he didn't know were there are gone. The only wall that remains is David's.

Michiko's Garden

Very Sexy Vegetables

Michiko

Michiko is my neighbor in the community garden and to get to my garden, I must walk by hers. It is lush and abundant, planted from border to border with an astonishing variety of flowers and vegetables. I see her garden nearly every day—and then again, I don't.

Because Michiko is a photographer, she has a unique lens on the world. So when I walked into the gallery where she sells her work, there was her garden on the walls all around me, but altogether different. Her peppers no longer were hanging on the plant; instead, one recognizable long red pepper and one long yellow pepper were entwined in a passionate embrace in a photograph titled "The Lovers." Her okra no longer bore any resemblance to the long, green vegetable that grows in the rest of our gardens; by cutting it in cross-sections, she revealed its basic star shape and named the composition "Stars." Nearly all who look at the photo assume they are looking at star fruit. Michiko's sunflower was really a half sunflower, shot so close up that the petals were brilliant rays of sunlight bursting up from the bottom of the photograph like a morning sun coming up over the horizon. Strawberries sliced paper thin and backlighted were playfully arranged in a composition called "Dancing Strawberries."

Michiko plants her garden with her photographs in mind, and then that mind transforms the ordinary into the extraordinary. She gives those of us who garden with her a new perspective on our gardens and the gift of better knowing the vegetables and flowers we grow. She also nourishes the souls of thousands more people with her photographs, as the abundance of her talent and the beauty of her garden go far beyond the fence that encloses it.

Michiko's Garden

VERY SEXY VEGETABLES

I came to the United States from Japan to work for an international organization in Washington, D.C. I liked my job, but I couldn't stand the internal politics, so eventually I left and found my way into photography. Photography had been a hobby of mine, and when I left my job, I enrolled in a nearby college and earned an arts degree in photography.

One summer when I was a student, I walked by the community garden. Everything was blooming and I asked one of the gardeners if I could come in and take photos of the sunflowers for an assignment. The photos I took that day are very different from the photos of sunflowers that I sell now, because I was just a student and did not have my own style yet. When I finished taking pictures, I asked the gardener how I could rent a plot. He told me and I began to garden here 13 years ago. I'll tell you, it's a lot more labor intensive to grow a garden than it is to take photographs! I win awards for my photography, but I think I really deserve an award for working so hard in my garden.

Most people take pictures of things straight on. But if you do that, a strawberry is just a strawberry, and it does not show what I see. I try to express the beauty of my subjects the way I see them.

Before I had my garden, I used fruits and vegetables that I could buy in the grocery store. I started with strawberries and okra. Then one day a friend called me and said, "Michiko, I saw your photos of strawberries and okra in a restaurant downtown." Only I didn't have anything on display at that restaurant. Someone had copied my style! I started gardening so that I could use fresh produce and plant unusual things that people don't have easy access to. Bitter melons, fava beans, and poppies are subjects that are harder for others to copy than bananas and strawberries.

Because there are twenty plots in our community garden, people assume that I take photographs of other people's gardens. I don't even take pictures in my own garden because of the way I do my photography. I think that lighting is the most important element in taking a photograph, and at the garden I don't have any control over the lighting. I take a lot of close-ups that require total stillness, and even the slightest breeze can ruin the focus. So I photograph my subjects at home. One of the best things about having a garden is that my flowers and vegetables stay fresh and last longer than store-bought. Of course, there is always much more in the garden than I need for my photography. What I don't use, I eat. My profession has inspired me to become a vegetarian!

I do lots of thinking before I take a photograph, and I look at the objects in relationship with each other. I did a series of pears a few years ago. I bought the pears at the farmer's market and at a few food markets, and it took me forever to choose just the right ones. The first photograph that I took was a single pear in which I saw the shape of a human bottom. Then I began to play with two other pears, a red one and a green one. I placed them right up next to each other, like an affectionate couple, and called that photo "A Pair of Pears." Then I noticed that two of the other pears looked a little beat up and tired, so I put a few drops of water on them, set them on a piece of white satin and named the photo "Pears—After the Loving." Another time, I saw a beautiful curve in a yellow pepper that reminded me of a woman's back. I turned it sideways on white satin, as if it were a woman resting on a bed, and called it "Pepper—Repose." My pear and pepper photos have been very popular. People seem to enjoy the humor and fun. I've even won prizes in photography contests.

This year I have 37 different vegetables and flowers in my garden, which is only half a plot—10 feet by 15 feet. I pack in as much as I can—cosmos, three different kinds of sunflowers, dahlias, gerbera daisies, asters, statice, stock, sweet peas, bells of Ireland, hollyhocks, marigolds, four o'clocks, and I love the blue of the morning glories. I have garlic, parsley, Chinese chives, and basil—I use basil all the time in cooking. Then there are the eggplants, tomatoes, carrots, and zucchini. The color of eggplant is good, but I haven't yet found one that's the right shape to photograph. I also plant some Japanese herbs and vegetables that are hard to find in markets. Shiso is an herb that has an appetizing aroma and lots of vitamin C. Japanese restaurants use it with sushi and sashimi; I wrap pickled herring in it. Weeds grow in my garden, too! When I was a child my mother made me weed her rose garden and I hated that. Now weeding is therapy. Whenever I have a problem, I just go to the garden and weed, and I come home feeling better.

Right now I'm in transition with my art. It isn't clear to me whether I will keep my style that I have now or go in a different direction. So my garden this year is different from other years. I'm not as organized, thinking "I should plant this and this and this to photograph." This year, I'm just putting things in and letting them grow. And I don't have to rush down to the garden to pick things on exactly the day they are perfect for the photograph. It's more relaxed this way—and perhaps it's the pause that always accompanies a surge in creativity.

Carol's Garden

A Palette of Colors

Carol

Carol and I are bonded through suffering. Both of us have had our gardens eaten down to the ground by deer. Both of us know how much it hurts to have what you have loved and labored over and admired disappear overnight. Neither of us are fans of Bambi!

When I first visited Carol in her new house in the Pine Flats of New Jersey, she had impatiens planted all the way around it and a beautiful English garden in the back. After her deer disaster, she vowed not to try again. But several years later, sitting at her kitchen table on another visit, I looked out to her yard and noticed that the flower boxes edging her deck were filled with bright red geraniums growing out of rich green foliage. "You decided to plant flowers this year?" I asked. She laughed and took me to the deck. The foliage was real—an old-style vinca which deer don't like—but the geraniums were silk. "I couldn't live without the color," she said.

Carol is a watercolor artist and her paintings blaze with strong, bright colors. Luckily, she had painted her garden before the deer made a midnight meal of it. She's lucky, too, that she has a beach house on the New Jersey shore and a garden there where the deer don't roam. It's not as large as her other garden—in fact, it's tiny—but it is brimming with bright colors to paint.

Carol has lived on or near Long Beach Island most of her life, and you can't walk a block beside her without someone calling her by name—an island neighbor, a student from one of her painting classes, the owner of one of the galleries that display her art, a friend from one of the many volunteer projects she's involved in, or the owner of one of her paintings, who stops to tell her how much she is enjoying it in her home.

I own several of her paintings myself—sand dunes, ocean, and bright, cheerful gardens that make me smile every time I walk by them, especially in the dead of winter.

Carol's Garden

A PALETTE OF COLORS

They say you have to do a thousand paintings before you're a good artist. I'm sure I've done a thousand paintings, so I guess that means I'm good! At least a third of my paintings have been florals. My garden. Other people's gardens. Individual flowers.

I majored in art in college and then taught art, but I didn't do any gardening. Then I had two babies and began to garden, but I didn't do any art. By the time the children were toddlers, it felt like everybody was taking a piece of me and there wasn't anything left for myself. So I decided to take a watercolor class at the local art center. I loved it, and when it was over I asked my teacher, "What do I do now?" She said, "Go home and keep painting." I set up my studio in the basement playroom and the children played while I painted. After a year or so, I felt it was time to do a show. That summer, I was one of the artists in our town's Festival in the Parks. I hung my paintings on the fence with about 100 other artists and started selling. That was in 1976 and I've been doing watercolors ever since.

I am basically a colorist. I love a lot of color in my paintings, so I plant a riot of color in my own garden. Some of my friends do their

gardens in shades of pink, some in yellows and blues. But I like hot
colors and no rows. Everything tumbles and mixes together.

My love of color is what led me to paint other people's gardens. I would be driving around town and if a garden caught my
eye, I would walk up to the house and say to the owner, "You have
a beautiful garden. May I paint it?" In the beginning, I would take
photos and paint at home. When the children got older and I had
more time, I would go right into people's yards and set up my
easel. I really enjoyed that; it was fun to talk to the gardeners.
When I showed my paintings at art shows, people would say, "I
have a pretty garden. Will you come paint it?" So I started doing
commissions and word-of-mouth led to lots of work in lots of
beautiful gardens.

Another getaway that I thoroughly enjoyed during those early
years was painting at a local nursery down a country road not too
far from my house. They raised all sorts of flowers in their hot-
houses—roses, gloxinias, poinsettias. I would take my stool and
easel into the hothouse and paint. Sometimes I would do a tight
focus on one particular flower or sometimes a whole arrangement.
The old farmer who ran the place was a dear and he let me move
the pots around and arrange them however I wanted. I loved
painting there—the brilliant colors, the warmth, the perfume of
the flowers.

One of the most memorable gardens I've painted is Eleanor's
garden. I met her at an open house to support historic preservation
here on Long Beach Island. She was 80 years old and had gone in
costume—a 1925 bathing suit with a bathing cap. We began talking about plants and gardens and she said, "Come see mine." So I
did and I was enchanted by her 100-year-old cottage and the

"secret garden" behind it. At the end of the visit, she invited me to come back and paint. I took all my painting gear and painted for hours in her beautiful garden. What a delight!

By now I was teaching watercolor classes myself. Since it was summer, I was teaching an outdoor painting class. I asked Eleanor, "How would it be if I brought my class over to paint your garden?" She loved the idea, so the next week eight people scattered all around her little yard and painted her flowers and vegetables. I did that for three summers, then I had an idea. I had always wanted to go to Monet's garden at Giverny in France. I thought, "Well, I can't go to Monet's garden right now, but I have Eleanor's garden right down the street. And I can invite people to see the paintings of it."

So I found a nice gallery space and contacted all my students. I told them they had until the next April to paint Eleanor's garden for the show. They could go back to the garden or use photos. I encouraged them to paint the garden in all seasons. The show opened the next spring and was a great success. Each of the 15 artists showed two or three pieces. Of course, Eleanor came to the opening and she was thrilled. The newspaper featured her in a lovely article. Over the years, I've continued our friendship, visiting with her and painting in her garden. My life is so much richer for all the people I've met through gardens and painting, especially Eleanor.

I use flowers from my own garden in my paintings, too. My garden at the beach house is tiny, but I fit a lot in it. Petunias, portulacas, cosmos, impatiens, rudbeckia. I plant milkweed because the flower is a magnificent sphere, sometimes up to six inches around, with tiny lavender flowerets that are so sweet they attract bumblebees in big crowds. When the flower dries up and falls off, the pod develops and I love to paint milkweed pods. I keep some dried pods in my studio and every once in awhile their little seeds float around as I paint. I plant blue catnip because we have a cat that likes to play in the garden. And I always grow goldenrod because that's a major plant food for the monarch butterflies that migrate in the fall along the coast on their way to Mexico. They like the October daisies, too. So there's always plenty of color for me to use in my paintings. Living next to the ocean, I also use seaweed as a subject. It's a flower, too—a water flower.

I paint what I see around me, and I try hard to really see and know what that is. I tell my students they need to develop the Zen of seeing, that they need to study a plant and get to know the plant as a plant, just as they would try to get to know a human being.

From the time I was a small child, I've been intrigued and fascinated by small, beautiful living things. I would go out in the yard by myself and build little fairy kingdoms with pieces of moss and twigs and small flowers. My parents divorced when I was eight and when I was 12, my mother died of cancer. I think I used my imagination to escape from all the sadness, used it as a tool to survive. Now, instead of building fairy places with moss and twigs, I use my imagination in my painting. And instead of it being a solitary activity to escape from others, my imagination and my paintings connect me to others.

Over the years I have become a very spiritual person. Not religious in the sense of being extensively involved in a church, but spiritual in the sense of realizing that God the Creator of nature and human beings is a wondrous, magnificent being. I see the wonder of God in every flower I paint. I have also seen that when nature works well, everything is in balance. In a garden, if there is too much water—or too little water—it's out of balance and does-n't grow properly. Observing my garden helps me to keep all the parts of my life in balance.

The weeds in my garden have also given me insight into life. Our tendency is to yank weeds out of the garden, throw them in a trashcan or compost heap, and be done with them. But some time back, I heard someone say, "A weed is just a plant out of place." In dealing with my own sense of rejection at times in my life, espe-cially as a child, I have felt like a weed. But those flowery little weeds that we think are in the wrong place are often quite lovely if you look at them closely. What I've learned in my garden has enriched my life, because now I have friendships with people that I might otherwise have passed over as "weeds."

One of the most rewarding aspects of my art is teaching. It is important to me that my students leave class feeling good about themselves and encouraged to continue painting, no matter what their level. One of my students has gone on to be a very successful watercolorist and that's really exciting for me. I know that is not the case for all teachers, because over the years I've had teachers who are threatened by their students. They think that if they tell too many of their secrets, their students might become so success-ful that they cut into their sales or take something away from them. That never concerns me because I'm always learning from my stu-dents. At the end of each class we do critiques and they see things that I don't see. My eyes are always being opened. I hope I don't ever get puffed up like a bullfrog sitting on a lily pad. I always want to have an open hand.

People often say to me, "How can you sell your paintings? How can you let them go?" But how many paintings can I hang on my walls? And if I keep them in a drawer, who does that serve? If I keep my paintings to myself, my life is closed. But if my art brings joy to someone's life, I feel good. As long as my hand is open to give, it will also be open to receive from others.

Eleanor's Garden

A Garden for All Seasons

Eleanor

I met Eleanor when I went to visit my friend Carol, who lives on Long Beach Island in New Jersey. "You have to see Eleanor's garden," she said. Then she picked up the phone and 30 minutes later, I was standing in front of Eleanor's house. She lives in a little brown clapboard cottage that was built in 1908 and is now one of the island's designated historic buildings. It is surrounded by a border of tall pines, which gives it an intimate, tucked-away feel on this barrier island that is flat, sandy, and mostly treeless. Even more surprising is the garden itself. Walking into Eleanor's garden is like being served a seven-course banquet when all you were expecting was a sandwich. It is a hidden jewel, a 30 x 40-foot plot that is as enthusiastic about life as Eleanor is.

In her late eighties, Eleanor is the octogenarian every woman hopes she will have the good fortune to become. She is sharp-minded, completely comfortable with her life, utterly curious about everyone and everything, and still filled with wonder at the beauty of the natural world that we humans are privileged to enjoy.

For many years, Eleanor has given historic tours of the island on the Jolly Trolley. The morning I met her, one of her passengers was a 14-year-old boy. "He looked at me as if he thought I was just a shriveled-up old thing. Then I opened my mouth," she recounted with a twinkle in her eye that left no doubt she had changed his mind. To make sure that we, too, knew exactly how she felt about life, this former English teacher and lover of literature pulled up a line from one of her favorites, *archy and mehitabel*: "there's a dance in the old dame yet, what the hell, what the hell."

Eleanor's Garden

A GARDEN FOR ALL SEASONS

I call my house Halligenlei. Out in the North Sea, there are little islands. Some of them are inhabited and some of them are too tiny for a house, but some are just big enough for a house and a barn. In Gaelic, that's called a hallig. A house or shanty on a hallig is called a "lei." So a halligenlei is a little shanty on an island that has no protection from the sea. I visited a halligenlei once and said, "That's what I shall name my cottage." Of course, today there are houses all around mine, but I imagine when this little house was built in 1908, there were very few others on the island. So this is my halligenlei, my cottage with a garden on an island in the sea.

My love of gardening came from my love of being outdoors. Every Sunday when I was a little girl in the early 1900s, my father took me out driving and introduced me to flowers. He tested Mercer automobiles and each Mercer was made to order, right down to the colors and the owner's initials painted on the car. The cars had no top and a front seat only, and off we would go to test them, riding along side by side in the sunshine. It was wonderful!

One day when I was about three or four years old, my father

pulled over to a place where there was a bit of moisture and a pretty orange flower blooming. "See all those spots?" he asked. "Can you guess the name of this flower?" When I couldn't, he told me, "It's a tiger lily." And that's how I learned to call flowers by name. It's such a shame that they cut the grass on the roadsides these days. It used to be that you could just stop the car and pick big bouquets of lovely flowers. Everything was so pretty.

It was on one of these Sunday outings that my father first brought me over the clappity wooden bridge to Long Beach Island. Forty years later, in 1954, my husband and I bought our cottage and we started coming here in the summers with our two boys. And even though it wasn't until the early seventies that we moved here permanently, we began right away to work on the yard.

We knew we wanted trees around the house, so I found a nice lady who sold Japanese black pines and she came out and planted them. When we moved here for good, the pines were all grown up and waiting for us. After we moved in, we planted a little blue spruce that's taller than the house now. And we "encouraged" the big cedar that's by the mailbox. I love the blue berries and green leaves of the cedars, so I kept a bouquet in the house one winter. In the spring I thought, "Time to throw it out." And from that throw-out grew the big cedar tree that's so pretty now. I learned that they grow very easily in the sandy soil here. So do beach plums, which is why I have so many around my house. My neighbor was a gardener and he said, "Eleanor, anything that volunteers to grow here, give it a chance, because this is a hard place to grow anything." I've made beach plum jam every year since I moved here. I love the burgundy color and the flavor is delicious.

The boys and I thought about having a garden right from the

beginning. Out in the backyard I strung a clothesline in a square on four poles. Then we put down a wooden path around it for me to walk on when I hung up clothes. My son looked at it and said, "Mom, we should have a garden inside the square." So I got the name of one of the old-timers on the island who hauled sand and I called him up. A few days later he pulled up in a big truck, took out all the sand and put in this good earth. My neighbor came over and picked up some of the soil and smelled it. "Ahhh," he said, "pigs! This is going to be good." And it has been a very good garden indeed!

I never dreamed of having that big a garden. But once the soil arrived and I began to plant in the square, I needed a fence to protect the flowers from the wind. My neighbor gave me some more good advice: "Don't get a fence that's too tight. Leave an inch or two between the boards, so when it gets hot you'll have some ventilation." Other times he would come over to the back door and call, "Anybody home? Time to pick blackberries!" We'd all grab our pails and off we'd go. He's gone 20 years now, but he was a good neighbor.

He gave me a lot of tips, but I don't think it's a wise thing to take too much advice about your garden. When I first started, one of my favorite books was *How To Have a Green Thumb Without an Aching Back*. The author says she has found that people who have gardens are very willing to tell others how to do theirs. But she encourages gardeners to experiment for themselves. Goodness knows, I've experimented in my garden for the last 55 years. That's how I've figured out what I should and shouldn't do. A garden is a lot like life—the best way to live is to live it!

I like a garden where something is always happening, so I try to plant things that will bloom or ripen in succession. I've kept a journal, month by month, for the last 28 years.

In January, there's Scotch heather in the back yard. I thought it wanted good soil, but it just took hold in the sand and began to grow. The blossoms are dainty little pink and white things, quite inconspicuous. Toward the end of January, I begin to see the migrant birds coming north. The primroses begin in February. That's what I enjoy the earliest, with all their bright yellows and pinks and purples. This is also the time to lime the garden and spread the horse manure.

I know that March has arrived because the laughing gull with its black head returns. The herons come back and the hawks are courting. Crocuses poke through in March and the first rhubarb comes up. It's beautiful to watch a rhubarb plant form its leaves, with everything wrapped up in a tight, shiny red and green knob. The radishes begin to show and out on the sand flats the pyxies bloom so pretty in pink and white. The spinach comes up and one year I planted tatsoi, a Japanese herb. I've tried lots of lettuces and greens—what's the fun of a garden if you aren't trying new things?

My garden really comes alive in early spring: daffodils, narcissus, hyacinths, bleeding hearts, and columbine. The daylilies come a little later. Out on the Pine Barrens everything is coming to life, too. Asphodel. Arethusa. Starflowers. And now the purple martins come back and fill both of the birdhouses in my yard.

In May, I plant most of my vegetables, and I do it according to the moon: "If it's down, you're down." Anything that grows underground, I plant at the down of the moon, when it's dark— beets, carrots, potatoes, and the like. What grows above ground, I plant at the full of the moon—lettuce, tomatoes, red and green peppers, eggplant, and much more. Late in May the foxglove blooms. By that time the finches are back. So are the grosbeaks and the hummingbirds, and the wisteria is loaded with blossoms that fill the air with perfume. I like to take spring walks down to Great Creek Bay, where I find toadflax and Venus fly-traps. If I see the goldfinches gathering thistledown, it's a sign that they're ready to build their nests.

Then the summer flowers start blooming. I plant different things each year—miniature zinnias because they're so good for bouquets, cosmos, marigolds, lobelia, geraniums, pussytoes, petunias, carnations. The butterfly bushes bloom and black-eyed Susans fill one corner. I once had a gorgeous white Datura lily that bloomed at night. And out in the Great Swamp in early August, the lovely yellow fringed orchids bloom. They're protected—you daren't touch them.

The first year I planted potatoes, I didn't know you have to put the eyes out. I just cut up potatoes and put them into the ground in pieces. When I dug the potatoes up, I had the whole Mickey Mouse family. The potatoes all had heads and tiny little ears! I set them out in front of the house so people on their way to and from the beach with their children could see them. My potato family made a lot of people laugh and started a lot of good conversations!

You mustn't forget to feed your garden. It makes sense for me to use fish since I live by the ocean. I just go up to the fish store and they let me take the heads and whatever other parts they discard. Years ago I had a big compost pile. Then I got down to having just a little pile. Now I put the table scraps right around the plants and put some mulch on top so I know the plants have been properly put to bed.

In the fall, I seed things. Whatever is giving its seeds at that time, I throw into a little patch of scratched-up dirt. In early November, I plant two rows of garlic so it will be ready to harvest the next summer. And there are still things to pick. Being next to the ocean keeps the climate temperate longer than inland. Raspberries bloom twice for me, June and November. There are still beets and peppers and leeks. The butternut squash hangs on through late fall, too, and it's fun. It grows long and looks like a club you could use to hit someone over the head! I split it length-wise and seed it, then bake it skin side up on a cookie sheet at 300 degrees for about a half-hour. When I serve it, I put some cranber-ries on top and it's pretty enough for company.

Then, before you know it, it's January. The birds begin to come north at the end of the month and the circle begins all over again.

My garden has always brought people into my life, some of whom have become good friends. But some years ago, a very spe-cial thing happened. A friend who is an artist asked me if she could bring her watercolor class to paint in my garden. "Of course," I said. For several years and in different seasons, Carol and her stu-dents came and painted. Then she mounted a show called "Eleanor's Garden" at a gallery here on the island. Seeing the paint-ings of my garden in all seasons made people realize that a garden can be pretty any time of the year. After the show, I had lots of peo-ple stopping by to see "the original."

As I walked through my garden with one of these visitors, I asked her if she had a garden. "No," she answered. "I live in New York City." The next week she stopped by again and said, "I just want to see what's growing in your garden this week." She liked arugula, so I sent some home with her. A couple of weeks passed and she asked me if it would be all right to bring her husband over. So he came and liked the garden, too. "Now it's your turn to visit our garden," he said. A few days later he picked me up and drove me up the island to see the flower garden in front of their house. Then we sat on the back deck and looked out at a lovely view of the dunes and the ocean. When their vacation ended, they went back to New York. But that fall, they invited me to spend Thanksgiving with them in the city. Now when they come down to the island in the summer, they pick me up for dinner and to watch old movies with them. They still like to visit my garden, too.

Friends asked me after the show if I minded having so many people stop by to see my garden. I didn't mind at all. It was wonderful, because the more people I can share the pleasure of my garden with, the more joy it gives me—a joy that just spills out into every other part of my life.

Francie's Garden

An Elizabethan Knot

Francie

Francie's garden doesn't look particularly interesting at first glance. There are not a lot of showy flowers and the plants in it are subtle. Then Francie walks in and the garden not only springs to life, it becomes a magic carpet that transports you back four centuries in time. Her garden is the Elizabethan Garden at the Folger Shakespeare Library in Washington, D.C. and, of course, it isn't really "her" garden. But it is her passion, and if you stop by on the third Saturday morning of the month, she will give you a guided tour. She will take you into the herb gardens and kitchens of Elizabethan England, when the lady of the house was usually the druggist to her family and keeper of recipes for medicines, perfumes, cosmetics, cleaning solutions, and insect repellents. She will take you on a tour through Shakespeare's works, written at a time when people were so intimately connected to herbs and flowers that his dozens of references to them literally constituted a language understood by all, rich and poor.

The garden is a 40 x 80-foot rectangle with two towering southern magnolias at either end. They are not authentic to an Elizabethan garden, but were planted some 65 years ago and are magnificent. In front of the magnolias, two benches sit on a path of white gravel that frames the garden. The lush green lawn that extends between the matching ends is interrupted in the middle by a 12 x 24-foot raised rectangle of boxwood, thyme, pinks, and rosemary arranged in a complex geometric pattern called a "knot." In the 16th and 17th centuries, many houses had herb gardens, but the wealthy planted their herbs and flowers in knot gardens and often created raised platforms so that viewers could better appreciate the design. The more intricate the pattern, the greater the show of wealth.

During the week, Francie is firmly planted in a 21st century classroom teaching English. While she is turning high school students on to Shakespeare, city workers spread out on the grass of the Folger garden at lunchtime to eat their sandwiches and weary tourists sit on the benches to rest their feet. The garden belongs to everyone. But on the third Saturday morning of the month, the garden belongs to Francie, with an open invitation to all to visit her there. As far as she's concerned, the more people who travel back to Shakespeare's England with her, the better the ride.

Francie's Garden

AN ELIZABETHAN KNOT

I arrived at the Folger Shakespeare Library at exactly the right moment. They had just begun to put in the Elizabethan garden in the late 1980s and none of the other docents were particularly interested in it. But I was fascinated. Fascinated to watch the knot garden take shape and fascinated to talk with the landscape gardener while he worked. I immediately adopted the garden as my baby. Then I started reading and researching, absolutely delighting in my access to the fabulous collection of books at the Folger Library. I turned first to Shakespeare and the plants that he mentions in his works. That led me to the whole realm of herbs, and I got involved in an exhibit based on a remarkable collection of rare herbal books owned by Mary P. Massey. Eventually, I started giving garden tours, which I love doing.

I have learned so much about Shakespeare just by looking at his plant references. Twenty-nine scenes in his plays take place in gardens and there are 150 references to plants throughout his works. Unlike most of his contemporaries, Shakespeare's references are very down to earth. Most of the other writers used stylized metaphors for plants and flowers that give you the impression they wouldn't have known a rose from a lily. Shakespeare talks about the ordinary plants and weeds that his mother and grandmother probably gathered on the banks of the Avon or in the meadows to use in cooking and medicines. It is a real country boy's knowledge of plants.

When you read Shakespeare's works, you discover that an Elizabethan audience would have actually recognized each individual plant and flower. For example, in Ophelia's speech where she hands out all kinds of plants and flowers, the audience understood exactly what each one symbolized. Rosemary for remembrance, pansies for thoughts. Rue, fennel, columbine, and each of the others had a meaning. Knowing the plant language opens doors to a much deeper understanding of his work and the times in which he lived.

In *Romeo and Juliet* there is a passage where preparations are being made for the supposed wedding feast between Juliet and Paris, and Juliet's father orders her nurse, "Spare not for the cost good angelica." For a long time, people thought the nurse's name was Angelica and that he was addressing her. As it turns out, the nurse's name isn't Angelica at all. Somebody put a comma where it wasn't supposed to be and capitalized that "A," making us assume that he's saying, "Good Angelica, go out and buy the best fare possible for the wedding." In fact, angelica is a root, and he is telling the nurse to buy good angelica, in other words, expensive candied angelica to go with the feast. It becomes even more interesting when you learn that angelica was used as an antidote to poison and poison becomes a theme later in the play when Juliet prepares to take the potion the monk has given her. All of this underlying tension in the text is lost on a modern audience because most people have no idea what angelica is. But an Elizabethan audience would have understood completely.

We have roses in the Folger garden, the white rose of York. There are 70 references to roses in Shakespeare, more than any other flower. And in *Two Noble Kinsmen*, Amelia says, "Of all flowers the rose is the best." Elizabethans used rose water for everything from food to medicine to cosmetics. It was traditional for women to collect the dew that gathered on roses, particularly on certain days of the year like May Day, and wash their faces with it, because they believed it made the face young again.

This was a time when keeping house was based on plants. A woman cleaned her house with plant material of some kind. There's a reference in *The Merry Wives of Windsor* about rubbing lemon balm on the furniture. Lemon balm smells like lemon and it has a lot of oil in it, so it was probably a primitive form of furniture polish. They put what they called "strewing herbs" on the floors of their homes. A poor person's house would have a floor of packed dirt, while wealthier people would usually use tile and occasionally timber. Either way, the floor was cold and they did not yet use carpets. So they put down dried reeds gathered from the edges of rivers and then sprinkled them with herbs. Walking on the rushes released the fragrance of the herbs, which was more a necessity than a nicety, since the rushes were only changed once or twice a year!

Herbs were sewn into the upholstery, too. They also put perfuming pans in the fire and burned herbs in them for the scent. What fascinates me is how we've come full circle, with the current popularity of aromatherapy. I recently read an article about a study being done to determine whether piping lavender scent into the office at four o'clock in the afternoon alters the brain waves of workers and increases their productivity. I'm eager to learn the results!

When you enter our Elizabethan Garden, there is rue growing on one side of the path and chamomile on the other. Rue was the symbol of regret. Medicinally, it was used to get rid of dandruff and as an ointment to treat eye diseases. Eaten with a fig and a walnut every morning, it was the leading herb used to ward off the Plague. Up until the first part of the 20th century, it was traditional to put a nosegay of rue on the benches of the judges in London court-rooms, a holdover from the times when they were afraid that judges would catch the nasty diseases that prisoners brought with them from the ghastly jails where they were held. John Gerard, author of the best-known English herbal in the 17th century, pre-scribed mixing rue with honey to "anoint the stones for swelling caused by long abstinence from venerie." In other words, an Elizabethan version of Viagra.

Chamomile was used for lawns and was mowed. It was also used on turf benches, because it was very hardy and released a lovely, apple fragrance. Chamomile was mixed with beer and drunk to relieve pain after childbirth. It was mixed with flowers and drunk to reduce a fever. Oil of chamomile was rubbed on the back for fatigue. And of course, Peter Rabbit got chamomile tea for his stomach ache!

At the entrance to our garden is columbine, a symbol of worth-lessness and infidelity in *Hamlet* when Ophelia hands it to Gertrude. The whole garden is enclosed in holly, which was very common in Elizabethan gardens. People usually tried to plant at least one holly bush near the house because they believed it attracted lightning and kept it from striking the house. The wood was hard and very fine-grained and was used for tools. It was so hard that there were actually laws that forbade people from using holly to drive their animals because it would bruise them. Holly leaves were used to treat fevers and colic.

At either end of the garden, we have hellebore, also called Christmas rose or Lenten rose. It's the most intriguing of plants because it blooms in the dead of winter. According to Gerard, it was used to treat "mad and furious men," as well as in a lot of household remedies. They steeped hellebore in wine to kill bedbugs, mixed it with barley and honey to kill rats and with milk to kill flies. It was used for epilepsy, melancholy, and you put it in your ear for three days if you were deaf. Combined with cooked apple as a suppository, it was used to induce abortion.

I wasn't very far into my research on herbs when I began to realize how much the women of that time knew about what we would call "reproductive health." I assumed that information about abortion would have been known by word of mouth, but I found dozens of references to remedies in print. Sometimes the author would use a euphemism like "to bring on the courses," but one chapter was simply titled "To Cause Abortion." Rue was used to cause abortion, along with germander and quite a few other herbs. What this tells me is that this topic was very much on their minds, and why not, when a woman was pregnant virtually her entire married life and stood a good chance of dying as a result of childbirth. They just looked at abortion as a procedure that was necessary at times. The problem is that the herbs that were used, both for abortion and other remedies, are often poisonous and therefore dangerous. We are so careful at the Folger to warn people not to try any of the remedies themselves from what they read at our exhibits.

Linden trees were commonly planted in Elizabethan gardens because they are very flexible and people used them for "pleaching," which means tying the branches together so that they form an archway. When planted by twos in pleached alleys, lindens formed a canopy of branches so dense that they could protect from both sun and rain. We have one linden tree in our garden.

English ivy, too, was common in Elizabethan England and was associated with alcoholic beverages because in ancient times it was connected to Dionysus, the Greek god of wine. Ironically, ivy was boiled in wine to cure a hangover caused by wine! It was also used as a depilatory when mixed with ant eggs, blood of lagoon frogs, and opium juice. I think today a preferred method would be waxing!

In the spring, daffodils bloom through our ivy. Daffodils were so plentiful in Elizabethan London that in the big Cheapside market, you could find women selling them all along the way. Gerard listed two dozen varieties in 1597.

The centerpiece of our garden is the Elizabethan knot. Elizabeth I came to the throne in 1558 and died in 1603, and knot gardens reached their peak during her reign.

A knot garden is a garden in an enclosed area, usually raised and planted with different plants that form interweaving patterns. Viewed from above, they are supposed to look like a piece of tapestry or embroidery work. One of the theories is that the knot gardens originated from the Elizabethan fascination with "Turkey carpets," which we would call oriental carpets, and the desire to recreate them with living plants. Some people say that the word "knot" refers to the knots that were made to create the patterns in the carpets, but there are other theories as well. These gardens were quite a fad at the time, and people of wealth vied with each other to see who could create the most elaborate design. Many of them were extremely complicated with coats of arms and lots of colors. Of course, gardeners did all the work. The fad didn't extend to the owners doing the gardens themselves!

Our knot is quite simple in design and is a closed knot, meaning that the area is completely covered in plants and there is no dirt visible. The trouble is that it's very hard to keep a knot going because plants have a tendency to die! Our knot is set off from the rest of the garden by a border of cobblestones. We also have a balcony so that people can truly appreciate what they're seeing, just as viewing stations were created for Elizabethan gardens.

We have both boxwood and germander in our knot. Germander is a member of the mint family and was used to flavor ale before folks started planting hops. It's called "poor man's boxwood" because it grows very quickly and was sometimes substituted for slow-growing boxwood to make edgings. Germander was one of the most common strewing herbs. Its medicinal uses were many: for melancholy and dim sight, for a stopped liver, for diseases of the brain, and against all poisons. Part of the fun of researching the garden has been to try to figure out exactly what a "stopped liver" was and what germander actually did in the way of a cure.

The saffron crocuses bloom in early fall. In Elizabethan times, people gathered the stigmas and roasted them over an open fire. It takes 100,000 blossoms to make one pound of saffron, which is why it is so expensive. In Shakespeare's time, there was a large saffron-growing industry, and saffron was used mostly for dyeing fabric and coloring food, rather than flavoring it. Saffron has a long list of medicinal uses, including a cure for jaundice. At that time, people held to a "Doctrine of Signatures," by which they believed that God made plants in such a way that the plants gave a clue to their use. According to this, liverwort is good for treating liver disease because its leaves are shaped like a liver. Saffron's yellow color indicated that it should be used to treat jaundice. Saffron was also considered an aphrodisiac.

The thyme in our garden is not the thyme that is used in cooking. We have creeping thyme, which grows low to the ground and forms a ground cover. It was also grown on turf benches because it releases a nice aroma when sat upon. In the Middle Ages, it was a symbol of courage and the crusaders' banners were embroidered with a sprig of thyme.

We have pinks in our garden, or dianthus, which are the precursor of the carnation. There were 50 varieties of pinks recorded in the 17th century and Parkinson, one of the well-known herbalists of the time, refers to it as "the chiefest flower of account in all of our English gardens." The color pink derives from the name of the flower, but not all pinks were pink. Some were white, others red, others variegated. Pinking shears, which cut with a jagged edge, were so named because of the jagged edge of the pink. In Shakespeare's time, dried pink flowers were used as a generic substitute for cloves because they have a strong clove scent and because cloves were extremely expensive.

Lavender is one of my favorites because it smells so lovely. It was a staple in the Elizabethan herb garden and was used both for washing clothes and for baths. They used it as a moth repellent by spreading their clothes out to dry on big lavender bushes so that the sun released the aromatic oils into the clothes. It also repels mosquitoes, so you can plant it strategically in your garden. In Shakespeare's time, they believed that lavender relieved headache and migraine, so they quilted it into caps "to comfort brains."

Finally, we have rosemary, which is a central part of our knot. There was a saying in Elizabethan times, "Where rosemary flourishes, the mistress rules." I love that! It is associated with fidelity and friendship and remembrance, as Ophelia says in her final speech before she dies. The list of uses for rosemary is quite long, from preventing disease to enhancing beauty. Leaves under the bed prevented nightmares and flowers placed in books prevented bookworms!

Of all the flowers and herbs in the garden, I feel the most personal connection with rosemary. It reminds me of my first herb garden back in the early 70s. I called it my "Simon and Garfunkel garden," because I planted parsley, sage, rosemary, and thyme. I laugh every time I think of it. I finally gave up on my herb garden because there just wasn't enough sun.

But rosemary also connects me to my mother and my roots. My parents are from northern Italy and, like many of the northern Italians who emigrated to America, they settled on the West Coast, in southern Oregon. The climate is so perfect for growing that my mother's rosemary bush is probably four feet tall and as big around. Every summer I go home to visit, and every summer my mother has started a little bush for me in a pot. I bring them home and plant them, but I just can't get them to grow in my yard because there's too much shade. Everybody thinks I'm crazy to baby these rosemary plants and I probably could do better if I went to a local nursery and bought a different variety. But there is something special about this rosemary plant. It is the same rosemary I grew up with 40 years ago and I really want it to live.

Strange as it may sound, I've come to know my mother better through my research on the Elizabethan garden. When I started reading, I was amazed at how familiar many of the remedies seemed to me. That's because some of them are exactly what my mother told me when I was a little girl. She was a firm believer in parsley for an upset stomach, and they certainly used that in the 15th, 16th, and 17th centuries. She cooked with lots of parsley and swore it was good for bad breath. Now, if you look on the label of some of the breath freshening products, sure enough, parsley oil is one of the ingredients.

My mother was born in 1907 in a small town in Italy and she came to this country in 1939, bringing with her plant knowledge that had been passed down for centuries from woman to woman in her family. As a child, I rejected it all. There was no way I was going to be like my immigrant mother. I was never going to make chicken broth; I was going to buy it in a can. But over the years, I've not only gone back to doing a lot of things her way, I've also come to appreciate them. Unfortunately, there's been a generation gap and I've lost something. I suspect my whole generation has lost something. That's why I require all of my students to talk with their parents and grandparents about their lives and write down what they learn in a story. Even if they save only one story, it's still one story that won't be lost to history.

When I give my garden tours, I hear lots of stories about gardens and remedies. Once I start talking about herbs, people want to tell me about something they're growing or something their grandfather grew or something they've read. I've taken people on tours inside the Folger Library. I show them our beautiful Great Hall. I tell them it's the kind of room they would have had in a big

Elizabethan house and I describe what they would have done in it. I tell them lots about Shakespeare. They listen politely, yet I rarely get any kind of interaction going. But on my garden tours, sometimes I can hardly get a word in edgewise. I think it's because when I give the inside tours, I'm talking about something static. No matter what I say, it still remains history and it's distant. The Elizabethan Garden is a different sort of history. It is tactile. People can smell it and touch it and it, in turn, touches them in a way that brings up a lifetime, or several lifetimes, of memories. Memories that connect them to their own past and memories that connect them, even as perfect strangers, to each other.

Beth's Garden

The Flow of Grace

Beth

Beth began our garden tour in her front yard at a piece of driftwood in the center of a small garden of purple impatiens.

"I brought this back from the lake a couple of weeks ago," she
bubbled excitedly. "If you stand here and look at it, you see a seal.
Look straight down on it and you see a cow's head with two eyes.
Over there it becomes an eel with its body wrapped around that
branch. Then here is a pig's head and there is some sort of fish. And
look, there's a horse. Isn't it wonderful?"

Beth is exceptional at seeing not only the hidden treasures in
driftwood, but also the hidden treasures in life. Perhaps that is
what helped her survive with such grace the four years her husband
Wade was dying of amyotrophic lateral sclerosis—Lou Gehrig's
disease. Her garden helped her, too.

Until the diagnosis, Wade was the family gardener, not Beth.
He spent a lot of time sifting and working the soil, and he planted
practical things like potatoes, tomatoes, and cucumbers. As the disease relentlessly robbed him of the use of his legs and arms and
their life closed in on them, Beth was drawn outdoors to the open
space of the back yard and the garden. Gradually but steadily, the
vegetable garden that Wade planted to nourish the body gave way
to Beth's garden, filled with the flowers and beauty she needed to
nourish her spirit.

Today, 15 years later, her garden takes your breath away. From
the street, Beth's house looks very much like all the other 1950s red
brick split-levels on the block. But when you open the side gate,
you step into a magical world, a hidden garden surrounded by

fences from which greenery cascades and sheltered overhead by a canopy of tall trees from neighboring yards. It is an enchanted land of pathways, benches, a pond and waterfall, fruit trees, flowering bushes, lush green groundcover, flowers, and little white lights that twinkle in the bushes at dusk. What you see is proof that hope can conquer despair, that life conquers death. What you see is the reflection of Beth's soul.

Beth's Garden

THE FLOW OF GRACE

I had always wanted a house where I could have a deck, but our house was built in the 1950s and it had a patio. Not just a patio, a super-duper 50s patio that was 21 feet long and surrounded by an ornamental cement block wall six feet high. Above that was a roof, which meant that we could use the patio rain or shine, but it also meant that the space felt dark and enclosed. We reached the point where I had persuaded my husband to look with me for a new house that either had a deck or space for me to build one. Then Wade was diagnosed with amyotrophic lateral sclerosis (ALS). Short of a miracle, we knew he wouldn't survive. So the plans for a new house—and my deck—were put aside.

Not too long after that, I was talking with one of my neighbors about wanting a deck and he said, "My son is majoring in landscaping in college. Why don't you talk to him?" I did, and within two months I had a beautiful two-tiered deck on the back of my house at a very reasonable price. It was a huge project, because first we had to dismantle the whole patio and cement-block wall. My husband was opposed to it, convinced that it would decrease the property value. But my spirit was crying out for openness. I said,

"We've had it this way for 11 years. How about we try something different?" And he agreed. Getting rid of that oppressive block patio felt like tearing down the walls of containment, the walls I had adapted to as the illness progressed. That act was also symbolically the beginning of my going it on my own.

Wade grew up on a farm in southwest Virginia and he believed adamantly that the soil was the most important part of the garden. He spent hours and hours and hours sifting the rocks out of the soil. He even bought a little sifter for our son when he was just a baby. Wade's approach to gardening was very practical, very utilitarian. Once the soil was improved, he planted potatoes, tomatoes, and cucumbers. He also planted Concord grapes and built an arbor that stretched all the way to the back fence. I planted some flowers in the front yard and the children had a swing set in a corner of the back yard. The rest was Wade's and I didn't bother much about trying to change anything. By insisting on the deck, I realize now, I was claiming my own way of being, honoring my need to create something beautiful.

The one thing we always agreed on was the fruit trees. Wade's family had fruit trees on their farm and my family had an orchard in their back yard. We both had a strong desire to grow our own fruit. Because the yard was not particularly large, we chose dwarf fruit trees. At least we thought we did. The two pear trees, the apricot, and the peach were dwarf. To our surprise, the apple tree turned out to be full size. In the end, what appeared to be a mistake has turned into an unexpected bonus because the apple tree is huge now and provides wonderful shade for a portion of the deck! In fact, nearly everything about my garden has happened unexpectedly.

I'm not a planner. I like to let things evolve. For example, I got my deck as a result of a random conversation. The flagstone path came to be because a friend offered to work with me. When I decided I wanted a pond, I went to a water garden shop and bought the fiberglass shell. I brought it home, and my teenage sons offered to dig the hole for it without being pushed or prodded, which is a small miracle in itself. Then a friend stopped by, saw the pond, and said, "Wouldn't it be nice to have a waterfall?" "Oh, I'd love that!" I said, and went out and bought some stones and a circulation pump. The following afternoon, he came back with the cement and put the whole thing together in two hours. The same thing happened with the lights on the walkways. An electrician came to repair the outside light on the deck, fell in love with my garden, and insisted that I needed low lights to illuminate the walkways. I bought them and he came back and installed them free of charge.

The whole experience—both Wade's illness and the garden— helped me grow to a deeper level of trust. I believe in prayer, and for me prayer is not petitioning to get something, but rather trusting in the flow of grace. Certainly that grace manifested itself in my garden as people appeared out of nowhere to help me create a space filled with beauty. Grace came into our lives in many other ways, too. People were always there for me when I had to face the next difficult task, like choosing equipment for the next stage of the illness or navigating the maze of insurance red tape.

Our boys were eight and nine years old when Wade was diagnosed, and I was working part-time. Wade wanted to work as long as he could, and even when his legs became paralyzed, he still had the use of his arms. So we modified our car with hand controls and he continued to go to his office. However, it took a full two hours, from 5:30 to 7:30 every morning, to get him out of bed, showered, dressed, and ready to go. It was exhausting for me to start my days that way, then get the boys off to school, then go to work myself. I prayed about it and a man's name came to mind. I called him, explained the need, and he said he would be glad to help. The next morning he came over at 5:30 and I taught him the routine. From that day until Wade was forced to stop working six months later, this wonderful man showed up every morning at 5:30 and took over. With his help, I was able to get up later, have time for meditation and centering, take care of the children, and maintain a sense of normalcy for the family. That's what I mean by trusting the flow of grace.

I did a lot of incremental grieving as Wade's capacities steadily diminished. As his muscles began to weaken, his gait became awkward and people would think he was drunk. This was very hard for him because he never drank alcohol. After that he used one cane, then two canes, then forearm crutches. He used a walker for a time, then he was in a wheelchair, then bedfast, then finally on a respirator. At various stages he would talk about the losses and not being able to do the things he loved. He grieved, and I grieved too, each time I saw another symptom, another regression, another exasperation. Then I would go out to the garden and plant things.

Working in the soil grounded me and reminded me in a tangible way of my belief in the oneness of all things—that the life force energy is everywhere, in leaves, in earth, in trees, everywhere. I don't believe in death. I believe that life continues on in another less visible form. For me, the garden was the unfolding of life, and that was very soothing. Planting and growing kept me very much in the moment, yet at the same time allowed me to work in future tense, planning and planting for next month or next season. The garden was therapy for me, symbolic of the new life I was beginning to create. There was a major loss taking place inside our house, but outside I was creating beauty, and most importantly, something that would continue to recreate itself.

I've planted everything that's now in my garden. I started with a landscaper, but the things he planted didn't do well. So I took them out and put in my own ideas. There was a rectangular space, so I put some rocks down, then planted some liriope and two azaleas. The next year I added variegated trailing vinca. I liked the azaleas so much that I planted bushes all the way around the garden. I chose them to bloom in sequence so that there is always color from April through June. The camellia blooms in March, the hydrangea in June. The rose of Sharon is a luscious shade of pink. The acuba over by the fence gives that corner of the garden a sort of jungle feeling. Most of the bushes that form the permanent portion of the garden were put in just about the time my husband went on a respirator and they were quite small. Now the pines and junipers and crape myrtles are far taller than he ever was!

My garden changes every spring. I try out annuals in different places from year to year and I put in new perennials. But the most fun is gardening with potted plants. Ten years after I had the deck built, I turned part of the upper level into a sunroom. It was a wonderful investment, the kind that just keeps paying me back because I use it so much. I eat out there, I have a Jacuzzi that I use year-round, and I'm surrounded by plants and flowers. When May arrives, all the plants come out of the house and into the yard. I dig holes and set the pots in the ground, then cover them with mulch. They look like they belong there, but I can tell you a lot of people are startled when they walk into my garden and see "jungle plants" like scheffeleras and ficus and poinsettias growing side by side with plants and flowers that are common in this mid-Atlantic zone. The best part for me about using my potted plants is that by picking them up and moving them I can essentially create a different garden every year—or change it midseason—without being ruthless!

Using potted plants also makes for low-maintenance gardening. Now, instead of coming out to the garden to work, I spend most of my time in the garden for other reasons. I've created five different areas for sitting. The cast-iron table and chairs over near the pond and waterfall are in a shaded area that is perfect for a glass of iced tea and a dish of mango with a friend. The chaise longue on the deck is my favorite place to read. I sit on the benches to be quiet and meditate. And I very much enjoy watering the garden, which is also a meditation for me. I love to come out early in the morning, around 6:30. The sun is just coming through the trees so that the water catches its rays and glistens. I love the reciprocity of the act, too. I'm taking care of my plants, and at the same time they're taking care of me, feeding my soul. I try to leave myself enough time for morning watering so that I don't rush through it and rob myself of the richness of the experience.

My garden is a spiritual place—and also more. It honors all three parts of myself. I actually have three names. My given name is Sara Elizabeth and people called me Sally when I was a child. Sally loves to play. She's the one who puts the wind chimes and pinwheels and windsocks around in the garden. Beth is what I have been called in my adult life. She loves to grow things and get her hands in the dirt. My spiritual name is Grace. She comes out here to sit quietly, to water, to meditate. All three of me love the garden.

During Wade's illness, he and I were both open to the possibility of a miracle, even though ALS is known to be a terminal disease. He didn't beat the odds, but we were blessed with many miracles. People appeared at every stage of the journey to offer help. The tiny seeds I planted blossomed into flowers. Bushes doubled in size from one year to the next and refused to be vanquished by winter. And my garden, my beautiful, sacred, whimsical garden, continues to be a powerful lesson for me in living a grace-filled life, in moving through the struggles and challenges, in trusting the peace that is always present—peace that is birthless, deathless, and never changes.

Zoe's and Julie's Garden

A Sea of Flowers

Zoe and Julie

Zoe's and Julie's garden is nearly three acres, a sea of flowers that is a feast for the eyes of the thousands of commuters who pass by every day on their way to and from work. Better still, the flowers are for sale from mid-July to mid-October. You simply make a turn off the busy road, drive back the gravel driveway about a hundred yards—and into a different world. On the left as you enter is a field of dahlias, so brilliant, so many colors that the intensity of it takes your breath away. On the other side, in a huge field, are blazing orange marigolds, a kaleidoscope of zinnias, pink and purple cosmos swaying in a gentle breeze, and long rows of golden sunflowers standing sentinel over all.

You park your car at the end of the gravel road and walk into a shady grove of trees. The tables, sheets of weathered plywood on stacked cement blocks, display whatever is in season—tulips, hyacinths, narcissus, azaleas, impatiens, petunias, chrysanthemums, poinsettias, or evergreen wreaths. In cutting season, bouquets fill the 50 or so coffee cans on the largest table and a hand-painted sign reads:

JUST FLOWERS
No delivery
No fancy wrapping
No vases, baskets, etc.
No designing or arranging

JUST FLOWERS
Fresh, good quality
Reasonably priced

Beyond the tables, two greenhouses fill the back clearing. The pigeons coo in their loft off to the left, chickens peck around your feet as you contemplate which spectacular bouquet of flowers to buy, and dogs snooze lazily in the shade. In a wooden booth, Zoe and Julie do their cash transactions out of an old plastic ice cream container.

The farm actually belongs to Stanley and Maria Mehr. They bought the land in 1951 so that Stanley, who is now retired from the U.S. Department of Agriculture, and his brother could indulge their passion—gladiolas and dahlias. Julie is their daughter and Zoe started working on the farm in high school so she could hang out with her best friend. That was 28 years ago. This is the only place either of them can imagine working.

If this operation were in the country, it would not be so remarkable. But it is just outside of Washington, D.C., fifteen minutes from the power center of the world. The farm is surrounded by large, expensive houses and occupies land that makes developers salivate. Yet these three acres are of another time, and this is what entices me and so many others in this fast-paced community we call home.

So do Julie and Zoe. I come to buy flowers from *them*, as opposed to just buying flowers. Because they have chosen to stay connected to the earth and its seasons, being with them makes me feel more connected. Because they have chosen to live life at a slower pace, I want some of their slowness to rub off on me. There are a number of different reasons why these two women have chosen to make this garden their livelihood, but they agree absolutely on one thing. "I could never have a job that keeps me inside," says Zoe. "Never!" agrees Julie adamantly.

Zoe's and Julie's Garden

A SEA OF FLOWERS

Zoe: I love to get dirty. When I was a child, my mom would throw me out the door in the morning and then open it at dinnertime for me to come back in! I knew when I got a job, it would have to be outside. I'd go absolutely crazy in an office. Now I'm over 40 and I still take my shoes off and walk through mud puddles. Sometimes I water the garden in my bare feet—mud up to my ankles. You can't do that in an office. You can't wear grungy clothes. You can't show up with dirt under your fingernails. I always wanted to be a farmer and live on a farm—and this is where I ended up!

Julie: My route wasn't quite as direct as Zoe's. I tried a few other things first, maybe because this is where I grew up and I had to do some exploring before I found my way back. I tried college and then went to England to work on a horse farm. When I came back, I worked part-time at this, along with other jobs. Then eventually I settled in. It really is a fun job because it always changes with the seasons. Actually, it's fun for a lot of reasons. I get to be outside. It's a busy job, but not terribly stressful. And I enjoy talking with the people who come in.

Zoe: So do I. Sometimes people come for no other reason than to talk and enjoy the flowers. It's much more laid-back here than in most of the other nurseries and garden shops in the area. You don't have to stand in line with people in a hurry behind you.

Julie: In the "olden days"—15 years ago—people would come out here and just sit in the back woods to relax. We had chairs and a picnic table back there. I've always felt a bit like a psychiatrist because people come in to talk about everything except flowers. Sometimes it's something sad, like a death or illness in the family. Sometimes they've come from shopping at the mall and just need to de-stress in a quiet place. Sometimes they're planning a wedding or party and ask for suggestions. I love the sense of community that we've created here.

Zoe: Some people just bring their children out to see the pigeons and the chickens and the dogs. You have to be a little hardy. Sometimes your shoes will get muddy and often the chickens are running around. And of course, depending on what season it is, we may not have time to talk at all.

Julie: From Christmas until the end of January, things are very quiet. Just about every other greenhouse in the area is closed. But we stay open—just to be stubborn, I guess. The rhythm is slow and we do a lot of organizing, cleaning our pots and the greenhouses, repairing, and replacing. At the end of January, the spring flowers start to come in. Primroses, tulips, narcissus, hyacinths. We keep them in the greenhouses, but when the days are warm—in the fifties or above—we put them out on the tables. I love that, all that bright color against the brown of the earth and trees.

Zoe: It's the cycles I love. We used to be a lot busier in the winter, when we grew more of the potted plants and bedding plants ourselves. Early in February, we'd go to the airport, pick up our geranium cuttings, and start planting them in the greenhouse. Geraniums are a big job. You take a sterile knife and cut off a growing tip on the geranium, or you buy the cuttings. You put them in sterile soil, water them, add a little lime, and fertilize them. When they get going, they just grow straight up unless you pinch out the leaf bud, which you have to distinguish from the flower bud. We pinched out thousands of leaf buds so the plants would branch out. And we hoped for lots of sunny days so the plants would get nice and bushy. If geraniums don't get a lot of sun, they get tall and leggy. Nowadays, you can use growth retardants and other products that make them branch out, so I don't think it is as much of a challenge to grow geraniums as it used to be. Nor is there as much of a connection with nature. You used to be able to look at the geraniums and tell if the spring had been sunny or cloudy. Today, they all look the same, so I don't think the consumer fully understands the connection of the plant to the weather and to the earth. It's like going to the grocery store and being able to buy strawberries year round, as opposed to when I was a child eagerly waiting for strawberry season. It's a degree of separation from the natural world around us.

Now we buy potted geraniums from a grower and this makes life a lot easier for us. I can even travel in the winter and enjoy myself! I remember taking a cross-country trip with a friend one January when we were still growing our geraniums from cuttings. When I got to California, all I could think was, "The cuttings are coming. I've got to get back!" You can get so caught up in the growing cycles that they determine your whole life.

Julie: It wasn't just the geraniums. We grew primroses and begonias and pansies and impatiens. We just got so busy we couldn't find the time to water the seeds and grow the plants properly. It's less expensive to buy the plants from growers and they have such a longstanding relationship with my father that we get top quality plants. So it's better this way.

Then in April, things really start to get crazy. Not only are people coming in for Easter flowers, it's azalea time. After that comes Mother's Day and bedding plants, so that by mid-May, we can hardly remember how quiet it was in January! But we've done this so many years and have gotten so good at it that even at the busiest moment we don't get stressed out. Tired, yes. But not stressed.

Zoe: When mid-May comes, it's time for us to start planting our fields. We used to plant most of our seeds directly into the ground—zinnias and marigolds and cosmos—but so many of them have been washed across the fields and into the stream by the huge downpours and thunderstorms we get in this area that we are starting more and more of our flowers in flats. The cockscomb seeds are so incredibly tiny that we always start them in flats in the greenhouse. But they are very demanding. As soon as they pop up, even if it is right in the middle of the Mother's Day rush, we have to get them outside immediately. Otherwise, they get tender and soft from being in the greenhouse and they blow right over on a windy day. They're like children—if you spoil them too much, they won't learn to thrive on their own.

Julie: This is also the time for the biggest job of all, which is planting the dahlias.

Zoe: Actually, it may be a bigger job in the fall to take them up. There are hundreds of dahlia bulbs, maybe thousands, and it takes us about a month to dig them up and put them in the root cellar. Julie and I dig them up, Stan divides them. Then we put them in crates and put moist peat moss on the top, and a piece of plastic on top of that. Then we carry them down to the root cellar. In the past, everybody had a root cellar, where the temperature stayed cool and constant through the whole year. We put the crates on high shelves because of a flooding disaster we had years ago after a big rain. Some of the bulbs we plant are actually from the original dahlias that Stan and his brother planted in the 1950s. Growing dahlias is almost like a sport. People who grow them take it very seriously!

Julie: In the spring, we put all those hundreds of bulbs back in the ground. And then we plant the field flowers. Some crops we put in later, and more than once, like sunflowers. Zinnias and marigolds will just keep going and going if you deadhead them. And we're always fighting off different kinds of insects. When my father started the farm, he planted fields of gladiolas, but we can't grow them anymore because of the Western thrip—an itty-bitty bug that gets into the petal and ruins every flower by making lines on it. We used to grow iris, but the iris borer put an end to that. We did asters for many years, all different kinds of asters, but they get soil-borne diseases that make them very difficult to grow. We try to rotate our crops. But sometimes a bacteria gets into the soil and there's just nothing to do about it. So we're forced to give up for awhile. It's always something.

Zoe: We avoid chemicals—we don't like them. We'd rather stop growing something than have to spray it.

Julie: By now it's mid-May. We're working seven days a week and we're exhausted. But no sooner have we gotten the plants into the ground than it is time to start weeding. You have to weed a lot in the beginning because the weeds grow faster than the plants, and if you don't pull them out, they'll shade the tiny plants as they come up.

Zoe: And, of course, there is Tshering, whom we couldn't do without. Tshering is from Darjeeling, India, and once worked on the tea plantations there at the base of the mountains. He is closely related to the Sherpas—small and mighty—and he works hard and steadily, not to mention that he understands plants better than he understands Americans! He came to the United States as a servant for a very kind man from the Indian Embassy and I remember clearly the day he came to us in 1987. He was looking for a place to plant a small vegetable garden where he could grow strange squash, bitter gourd, mustard, and other things he missed from home. He was making $50 a month and before he knew it, Stan was paying him $10 an hour to help us. If the spirits send gifts, he is one.

Julie: To me, he's a huge part of what makes Mehr Flowers what it is today. He's the bright light of spirit worked down deep into the foundation of our farm. Because of him, we're a blend of world styles. He also reminds us daily of all that we have to be thankful for. Like the weed. Tshering said one day, "Don't hate the weed. Without the weed, the plant has no value." And, in fact, Tshering does about 90 percent of the weeding.

Zoe: You don't dare to get behind in weeding with fields our size or you'll never get caught up. This is one of those things on a farm that just has to be done when it needs to be done, no matter what else is going on at that moment. But never if the ground has been turned and is wet. If you weed then, your shoes pick up the weed seeds and you end up planting weeds with every step you take. On the other hand, if one of us gets on the tractor and turns the soil between the rows of flowers on a nice hot day, those weeds will cook in the sun.

Julie: That's one of the nicest things about having a small business. We get to rotate jobs, which gives us all a variety of things to do. If Zoe feels like hopping on the tractor, she'll do some weeding or mowing. If one of us feels like being with people, we'll do the selling. If we want quiet time, we can weed or plant or water. We have soaker hoses that we can move around. If we have a drought, we just take the hoses and water and water and water. Staking and tying the dahlias takes hours of work—and miles of string. We just do whatever we're in the mood for.

Zoe: We cut the flowers in the evening when the sun is low or in the early morning. By the time we open for business, they are nice and crisp. When our cut flowers are blooming, from mid-July through frost, cutting is a huge job.

Julie: On a busy Saturday or Sunday in the summer, we sell well over 100 bunches of flowers. We start out with all the coffee cans and vases full of bunches of flowers and we just keep refilling them all morning. By early afternoon, everything's gone. Toward the end of the season, we have mostly dahlias. They come on strong in the fall, while we have fewer zinnias as the nights get cooler. Marigolds slow down. The sunflowers are over. There may still be some perennials. Each year we have fun choosing from the catalog different wildflowers for cutting and we plant them in a part of the field that is our perennial patch.

Zoe: The chrysanthemums tell us fall is coming. We don't grow them, but in August we start getting truckloads of them. Every color imaginable. In late October and November we dig up the dahlias and we plow the fields. Plow in the fall, turn in the spring. Fall is when we take care of our soil—there is nothing more important than the soil. If you keep using your soil without building it back up, you ruin it. We're constantly putting nutrients back into the soil. Julie and I both have horses, so we use lots of manure. That's the best! But wood chips are good, too, and leaf mulch. My grandfather was an impeccable gardener and he taught me to respect the soil. That's where it all begins.

Julie: Then come the holidays. We clear out the chrysanthemums and fill up both greenhouses with poinsettias. We sell Christmas trees and greens and poinsettias for the four weeks between Thanksgiving and Christmas. The whole farm is red and green for a month. Just spectacular. Then it's over for the year.

Zoe: I love to watch the seasons change—not just watch, but be a part of it. I feel very lucky to have a job that enables me to be so close to the cycles of the earth. And I love that I can bring my dogs to work with me. Sometimes I even bring one of my horses and let him mow the grass for us. One day I put Bosley in the dahlia field to "weed" in between the rows. I thought I had him closed in, but when I went to get him, he was all the way out front, eating grass on the roadside. It was rush hour and cars were whizzing through the intersection without even slowing down—not even the slightest curiosity about a horse standing beside the road. I thought, "What has this world come to?"

Julie: Horses are one of the reasons—the big reason—that Zoe and I live out in the country. She commutes 45 minutes and I drive an hour. I used to think I'd rather be working with horses, but not anymore. I don't think there's anywhere else that I could find the same kind of "family" I've found through the farm. We've gotten to know so many of our customers so well over the years that it feels like we are all one big extended family and this connection is very gratifying. Plus those of us who work together are just like a tight-knit family. We have some truly hard work to do, and of course, sometimes we disagree and have conflicts. But we have fun and freedom of expression as well—like the time Zoe brought in an old brass bed she had bought at a yard sale. She filled it with flats of pansies in every color of the rainbow, set it up near the entrance to the farm, and hung a hand-painted sign over it that said "Flower Bed." Everybody loved it! All in all, we are lucky to be able to incorporate the different aspects of ourselves into our work. So many people have a great divide between who they are at work and who they are in the rest of their lives. Not us. I think that working here allows us all to be more whole.

Zoe: I agree. And Stan is the most wonderful person in the world to work for. He loves flowers and he loves people, and that's what his life is about. Because he and Maria are not trying to make a fortune, they are extremely generous. "As long as we make a dime an hour," Stan says. And sometimes I'm not even sure they make that much. It is really hard to be a farmer and survive, and they make sure that Julie and I are paid well. They've turned down any number of offers on their land that would be hard for most people to refuse. "What am I going to do with the rest of my life?" Stan asks. "Sit around and count money? And what would you girls do without the farm?" That's a good question. At one point many years ago, I did some gardening for other people. But I realized quickly that working in other people's gardens took away from what I had to offer here. So I stopped, because this garden is where my heart is.

Mary's Garden

Doing What Comes Naturally

Mary

You have to look harder at Mary's garden than you do at most others. Sometimes you have to get right down to the ground to see it. That's because wildflowers are often small and understated, and wildflowers are most of what Mary grows. Actually, her passion is native plants, and that includes flowers, shrubs, and trees.

Before Mary took me on a tour of her garden, she took me for a walk. It was a sunny day in late February, the temperature had soared to a rare 70 degrees, and she wanted to show me something spectacular near her home. That "something" was crocuses, thousands of them making a carpet of purple across most of a large, shaded yard. It was so spectacular that when we stepped out of the woods and came upon it unexpectedly, I gasped. Then I got down on my knees to really see.

"Look," I said. "Some of the petals are white on the outside and some are purple."

"Botanically," she answered, "the key is that half of these are sepals and half are petals. Sepals are often green, but these are as colorful as the petals."

"What's a sepal?" I asked, revealing my appalling ignorance of the details of flowers.

Mary told me about sepals and petals and corollas, about monocots and dicots, and about how plants naturalize. At the end of this five-minute mini-lecture, she said apologetically, "That's a very amateur explanation."

To the contrary, it was fascinating. And it was the result of her lifelong interest in wildflowers and native plants, many classes, workshops, and guided tours, and more than 30 years of native plant gardening.

In her yard, Mary's love of native plants is manifest. She has to love them, because she spent hours yanking out runaway, invasive English ivy to make a place for what belongs. More than 75 species of native plants grow in her part-sun, part-shade yard and garden, from blue-eyed grass and wild geranium to pinxterflower and Virginia sweetspire.

Mary served as president of her state native plant society for three years. She has worked on statewide initiatives to protect and preserve wildflowers. She is so comfortable with the Latin names of plants that I often had to stop her and ask for the common name.

Yet she ended our tour by saying, "I'm still not a botanist." Then she paused and added, "But in my next incarnation, I may be." She *will* be. I'd put money on it.

Mary's Garden

DOING WHAT COMES NATURALLY

I think the first step to loving anything is paying attention. Many people don't pay attention to anything except people and perhaps mammals with big, soulful eyes. Anything green is just background and it might as well be plastic. But when you start paying attention to something, it is hard to keep from getting interested in it.

I've been interested in wildflowers since my childhood. I was what you would call a "highly supervised" child. One of my favorite places was a sort of no man's land beyond the edge of our yard, and I would spend hours out there by myself. It wasn't that I was doing anything forbidden or that my mother didn't know I was there. It was just that I felt free—there were fewer rules about "what we do" and "what we do not do" and "what you must do right now." Nobody mowed there and every spring a huge swath of purple violets covered the ground. I was eight or nine and I would go out and just sit among the violets. Then I would pick great armloads to take inside. It was such a pleasure to be out there with just the violets. Sometimes my father would take us fishing, but while he and my sister fished, I would go off and pick flowers. My love of wildflowers goes back a long way.

I grew up in central Illinois, went to college in Ohio, then to graduate school in New York City. I didn't learn a lot about wildflowers as I was growing up, I just knew that I loved them. When I was newly-married and living in Houston, we bought a tiny little lot on a tiny little lake about 30 miles north of the city. There was a variety of nice wildflowers on that lot and I decided that I wanted to get to know "my neighbors"—both plants and birds. When we moved back to apartment living in Manhattan, it was hard because I had no regular way of getting out into the country. After several years, we bought a piece of property and built a weekend house in northwest Connecticut. That's when I really began to learn about native plants—in my late 30s.

Our property was woodland, a stream valley that probably had not been disturbed for 60 years, and there were a lot of wonderful plants that I still miss. In fact, when we moved down here to Virginia, I brought some blue-eyed grass—which is a very small member of the iris family—because I didn't want to be without it, only to discover there was blue-eyed grass blooming along the edge of the woods behind our new house. A lot of the plants I loved in Connecticut are also found here naturally.

When we had our property in Connecticut, I took some workshops and guided tours to learn more about wildflowers. Then one year in the spring, I took a course in wildflower gardening at the New York Botanical Garden, which had a huge influence on me. The woman who taught it was tremendously knowledgeable. She had developed her own wildflower garden on Long Island, growing plants from seed or moving those the builder couldn't avoid into nursery beds. Then she planted them all among the trees in her yard so that instead of a few plants here and there, she had carpets of bloodroot and other wildflowers. People would visit her and say, "How lucky you are that all this just grows here naturally," with no clue that she had cultivated it. I thought it was really neat that she was able to emulate a natural woodland so convincingly.

I continued to garden with wildflowers in Connecticut until my husband was transferred and we moved to Virginia, just outside of Washington, D.C., in 1980. That was a terrible year, one of the worst I have ever been through. We had a lot of changes to get used to: my sister-in-law was dying of leukemia, our son was a sophomore in high school and was terribly uprooted, and I was having health problems.

One of the things that rescued me was an ad in the newspaper shortly after we arrived about a meeting of a fledgling organization called the "Virginia Wildflower Preservation Society." I thought, "That sounds like it's right up my alley," and I went. This was the beginning of my involvement, first as chapter propagation chair, then chapter president, then state president, with stints as newsletter editor along the way. During my tenure as president, we changed the name to Virginia Native Plant Society, having discovered that state agencies were a bit skeptical of small environmental organizations and tended to write off one with "wildflower" in its name.

At the time, a major issue was the flourishing trade in wild-collected plants and its impact on wild populations of plants that were greatly in demand and hard to propagate, such as trilliums. They grow so slowly from seed that propagating them usually isn't profitable for nurseries. So some nurseries would pay a pittance for hundreds of plants dug from wild populations, then resell them to an innocent public for maybe $5 a plant. The wild populations were being reduced, and buyers often paid well for plants that were severely stressed and might not live outside their native habitat. We did a lot of work to educate buyers to insist on nursery-propagated plants.

My involvement with the native plant society helped me through that very difficult time because it gave me a focus beyond all the obstacles and painful things that were happening at home. It gave me a place to belong, which I didn't have when I moved here. Working with wild plants helped me make this house and yard into something I was pleased with, and some of the plants I planted were those I had loved in Connecticut, so I still felt in some way connected.

Actually, I felt quite connected because I'd brought as much of my garden with me as I possibly could, both natives and other plants. That amounted to 40 pots of perennials! Let me paint the picture. When we came down for the closing on our new house, my husband's company put us up in a good hotel, all suites. We pulled up in front of it in our station wagon and the bellman brought out his cart, expecting a couple of suitcases. Then Ted and I started unloading pots. Five, 10, 20, 30, 40. I didn't even look at the bellman; he obviously thought I was mad. We took them up to our suite and put them on the Formica counter in the kitchen. A little later I realized I smelled gas from the range, which was bad news for the plants—probably for us too, but I was more concerned about my plants! I called the hotel manager, who told me soothingly that there is always a slight smell of gas with a gas range. Having cooked on one for 20 years, I wasn't buying that, but the bottom line was that he wouldn't do any-thing. So until we closed on the house and I could take everything to its new home, I kept the windows wide open despite the air conditioning. Then of course I had to load all the plants back onto the bellman's cart and put them back into the car. It was the same bellman and he still thought I was crazy. All but two of the plants survived this adventure.

Some of the plants were from my mother's garden, and some of those had originally come from other people's gardens. My mother had a border of bearded iris all the way down her driveway. They had come from her mother's garden because one of her neighbors in Denver bred bearded iris and gave my grandmother his extra tubers. But of course, there's a long tradition of plant sharing in this country. When I was growing up in the 30s, there weren't all the books we have today on gardening and there were fewer nurseries for ordinary people. Gardening was much more something that was done by professional gardeners for wealthy clients. Ordinary folks got plants and advice from friends and neighbors, especially during the Depression.

My mother didn't make a distinction between natives and non-natives, but some of the things she grew were North American natives. For example, she gave me a start of what she called sweet William from her garden. I later learned that its botanical name is *phlox divaricata* and it is native to a large part of the United States. Here it's usually called wild blue phlox. A lot of other familiar garden flowers were brought from the woods and meadows into gardens by early settlers.

Besides all the native plants in my yard, I also have about 50 non-native species. Most of the rhododendrons are not native, nor is the star magnolia. Evergreen azaleas originated in the Far East. The lavender one has huge flowers, and although lavender is not a color that I would have chosen for an azalea, this one was a gift from a friend who died a few years ago and I wouldn't take it out for all the world.

Some of the non-natives I put in mostly to conceal the fence our neighbor built. Then right in front of them I planted cardinal flowers, blue lobelia, white baptisia, and Virginia sweetspire, all of which are native. And there are native deciduous azaleas throughout the yard. The flame azalea is deciduous and came from a botanist in North Carolina who was doing research on propagating flame azaleas. He gave away the whips when he'd finished his project and I just happened to be visiting there at the time. I sat in the airplane with a tiny flame azalea in a three-inch pot between my feet all the way back to Washington. But it was worth it. Initially, I put the azalea in the ground where I had space, but it got too crowded. So I moved it and now it's doing beautifully. It's such a delight to look out from the breakfast table to this lovely orange-apricot azalea, and the chickadees, titmice, and Carolina wrens love to sit in it. It's quite a show!

I move things around a lot. I know it is sometimes hard on the plants, but I don't have a good design sense like some people do. I tend to put things in where I think they'll be happy, and if I don't like the way they look, I move them. But it's all part of the ever-changing nature of a garden. For example, one afternoon several years ago, we had a terrific thunderstorm and I actually saw one huge bolt of lightning hit five big tulip poplars. It scorched the bark of two all the way to the ground and the others suffered lesser damage. The next spring, none of them leafed out, so we had to take them down. Up popped a native holly that was just waiting its turn and a big patch of sunlight gave me more space for sun-lovers. Now I have thriving peonies—a wonderful Japanese peony,

"Krinkled White," and good old "Festiva Maxima," which is a very old variety that we had when I was a child. "Purple Dome" aster, a cultivar of the native New England aster, Siberian iris, a clematis, and stokesia are in there as well. The lightning strike made it possible for them all to do well in my garden.

Other things have changed, too. Down at the intersection about a half-mile from here, there used to be a 26-acre tract that was woods and an uncultivated field. Then the bulldozers arrived and took down the whole thing and a developer put up the most awful trophy houses. Shortly after they cleared the land, trouble began with the deer. We went away that year in late May. I have a lot of daylilies and they were more heavily budded than I had ever seen them. My hostas were looking wonderful. When I came back two weeks later, the deer had eaten every last bud of the daylilies and the hostas were nothing more than pathetic bare stems coming out of the ground. I was sick. I now spray the daylilies and other deer delicacies, and as I make changes, I'm trying to use plants they're likely to ignore. I refuse to let the deer take charge, and I'm trying to adapt to their presence.

The fact is, change is built into life and if you are going to be alive, you have to deal with change. If you're not able to change, you're dead.

That pertains to me, too. I'm not sure how long I will have the energy to keep digging and planting and moving things around. We have made a decision that we are going to stay in this house as long as we can, and I'm giving more thought lately to how I can make the garden more manageable for someone who is aging. I've had bouts with bursitis from time to time and I realize that I can't do the sustained hard manual labor in the garden that I could ten years ago. I've always tried to choose plants that don't require a lot of extra attention, and I've avoided the ones that should be lifted and divided frequently, like chrysanthemums. But there's still a lot of maintenance.

Over the last few years, I've begun to replace some perennials with shrubs, which need less constant care. There are wonderful flowering shrubs that are evergreen, and others, like the oak-leaved hydrangea, have lovely bark. When I do add perennials, I choose the ones that are long-lived and low maintenance. Peonies, for example, are said to go for 100 years with minimal care requirements. It also helps that I don't try to keep to a rigid design. If plants grow out of their space, I either rip them out or I let them grow over other things I care less about. In many ways, this garden is more casual and underdesigned than a lot of people would find acceptable. But I happen to like it and that's the whole point. The bottom line for me is that I'll take care of this yard and these gardens as long as I can. And when I can't, if I still want to dig in the dirt, I'll volunteer to work in a public garden.

The big pleasure of my garden is that it is a reminder of the way things are in the wild, and I find plants growing in the wild endlessly fascinating. Having a mostly native garden gives me the opportunity to encourage things to grow the way they want to. What I've learned in 30 plus years of gardening is that if you don't try to dictate to nature, it can do surprising and beautiful things.

Judy's Garden

Tilling the Soil of Friendship

Judy

If you were to phone Judy, chances are her husband would answer and tell you she isn't there, she's at the garden. Your next question would have to be, "Which garden?"

At her home, she has a lovely shade garden full of intriguing wildflowers. Since receiving certification as a Master Gardener, Judy has been a moving force behind two enormous volunteer projects: one at the Native Plant Garden at a nearby nature center; the other at her local library, where she and one other person have converted nearly a half-acre of lawn into an interactive, teaching garden for the community.

Then there are the "elder gardens," a little business she started to help older people keep up their gardens when they are no longer physically able to tend to them. To become one of Judy's clients, people must meet two requirements. First, the garden has to be of central significance to them, something that gives their spirits a sense of being alive. Second, the person must be able to move outside with her and tell her what he or she loves or wants in the garden, so that there is some sharing. In other words, Judy is not a lawn and garden service. She is a healer.

Finally, you might find Judy at her garden plot in the community garden. If she is there, you might also find me, because Judy and I are garden partners. For 12 years, we have turned the soil, planted, weeded, harvested, put up, given away, emptied our hearts to each other, laughed and cried together, and marveled at the miracles of the earth. Judy has an exceptional relationship with the earth, and through the earth, 30 years of relationships with a multitude of people. For Judy, gardens are all about friendship.

Judy's Garden

TILLING THE SOIL OF FRIENDSHIP

My first deep friendship with a woman was related to gardening. So for me, gardening and friendship go together.

Bonnie and I met at a Mother's Day Out program nearly 35 years ago and discovered that we both wanted a garden. She had a sunny yard; I had shade. I had a little gardening experience; she had none. So we teamed up that spring and planted our first garden at her house. The first thing we did—with her husband's consent—was to tear up most of the back yard and turn in the grass. It was quite a job—15 feet by 30 feet—but we were amazed at what happened next. The grass actually decomposed, as we'd read in a book that it would, and provided nitrogen fertilizer for the soil. Even though there was lots of grass and other seeds in it, we had an excellent garden that first year and could hardly wait until the next spring to start all over again.

We gardened together for ten years and it was a year-round enterprise. All winter long, Bonnie composted the scraps from her kitchen and turned the compost into the garden. We would get together and decide what seeds to order, what to plant where. We rotated crops and were constantly trying new things. One year we did pole beans, another year it was bush beans. We planted different kinds of corn and I've never been able to get cucumbers to grow like they did in her yard.

I look at my experience with Bonnie as a continuum. It started out because we both shared a love of working in the earth, and it evolved to a place where we shared so much of ourselves with each other that our lives became interwoven. We talked about our parents and our children and our husbands, our lives and hopes and dreams. For me, the turning of the soil and getting in touch with a sense of meaning in life are somehow interconnected. The tilling of the physical soil was also a tilling of the soil of our lives. Our caring for the earth was blended with our caring for each other, and for the stories that were brought up just by working the soil together.

We shared our garden for ten years and the end came very painfully for me one day in November when Bonnie called me out of the blue and said, "I don't want to garden with you anymore and I don't want to be your friend." I was totally shocked. There had been no warning that anything at all was wrong between us. It was so painful for me that to this day, more than 20 years later, I occasionally hesitate to pick up the phone for fear that I will get some message that just cuts me off at the knees.

Two years later, Bonnie committed suicide. From the day she called me, despite my attempts to talk with her, I only saw her one more time. She invited me to have lunch with her and brought me a big bag of vegetables from her garden. The conversation was, at least for me, careful. And that was it. We discovered after her death that she had systematically cut herself off from all of her friends, but had taken each of us out for some sort of a last meal and last conversation, although at the time we had no idea what she was doing.

Bonnie's suicide was so painful to her family that one of her daughters has recently made a documentary film called "Daughter of Suicide" in an effort to understand her mother and explore the feelings of those left behind. Depression and guilt, especially. As for me, I wonder if our gardening together made it so easy for me to share in her life and she in mine that there was some way in which the depth of her pain was hidden and that our sharing couldn't resolve it.

During the years I worked the vegetable garden with Bonnie, I became friends with another woman who taught me about wildflowers. I believed that because I had shade in my yard, I couldn't have flowers. But Janet taught me about all the shade flowers I could grow and she enriched my life immensely. She also got me started cutting flowers and bringing them into the house, which I had never done before. Neither my mother nor my father were gardeners and there were never flowers in my parents' house, so it never occurred to me to bring them in. What a delight it is to have vases of flowers in my home.

Though she readily shared plants from her garden with me, Janet and I rarely gardened together because for her the garden was a quiet place, a place to meditate, and not a time for sharing with someone else. Still, she is an important garden friend in my life and many of the plants that thrive in my yard are a reminder of our friendship. Celandine poppy. Jacob's ladder. Virginia bluebells. Cardinal flower. Black-eyed Susans. Evening primrose. Flowering quince.

Being cut off by Bonnie left me without a garden and without

a garden partner. Then a miracle happened—and truly, that is the
only thing I can call it. At the time, I was working once a month
with a spiritual guide. She and her husband, John, lived on a farm
about an hour out into the country. It was March and I was feeling
a bit sad about not having the garden to look forward to that
spring. "This is the first year I won't be planting peas," I said. Her
response was, "Talk to John before you leave." I did and that was
the beginning of my second ten-year garden partnership.

John was 72 years old when we began, an exceptional man,
deeply spiritual, extremely kind, a real gentleman. He was a former
Episcopal minister turned Quaker. He had been head of the
Institute for Spiritual Guidance in Rye, New York, then Director of
Programs at Pendle Hill Quaker Center in Pennsylvania before
coming to their farm in Virginia. When I met John, his Parkinson's
disease had progressed to the point where it was difficult for him
to take care of his garden. He needed help; I needed a garden.

Starting in April, I went every other week and spent a full day
working with John. We had an amazing relationship of ease, sharing the planting and weeding, sharing the times of quiet and the
times of talking. It was with John that I realized how much my
spirit was being enriched by working in the garden. For me, there
is a spiritual sense of the garden that I'm unaware of on a cognitive
level, a music and a sense of the plants' energy that permeates my
being, so that there is an ease in the way I move.

John saw this right away, perhaps because his first wife had
been a dancer. I would be thinning the carrots and he would say,
"You never waste a movement." Or when I was hoeing the beans,
he'd say, "You're so graceful." For awhile, I just pushed the comments aside and didn't really hear them. But he kept reflecting this

part of myself that I hadn't seen. Then he went even further by encouraging me to go to a week-long session with a woman named Barbara Mettler, an incredible dancer and teacher with whom his wife had danced. Barbara believes that everyone is a dancer and that dance is not about performance. I went to her workshop and it changed my life.

During that week, I realized how scattered I had become raising children, working part-time, being involved in the community. No matter what I was doing, it felt like I no longer knew how to concentrate at a deep level. Barbara's work is based on inner focus, where you are listening through your energy in a different way than I had ever done before, so that you never initiate a movement without allowing the energy to move you first. In other words, your response is always from the inside. By the end of the workshop, I was more focused than I had been for years—or perhaps ever—and I felt that I had movement capacities that I hadn't known I had.

John had seen it all along. He had seen the connection between the garden and the movement, and he gradually helped me accept that for myself. I had always thought of movement as being about steps and I don't learn sequences of steps very well. But this week was the beginning of my finding the mover/dancer in myself. I also began reading voraciously about the energies of plants and how they communicate with each other. I sense that I am very, very supported in the garden and I think that what John called "graceful" was movement supported by a kind of energy and music of the garden. From this point, I went on to get a Master's Degree in movement therapy. I love working with people, but I often find that helping them find the dancer in themselves takes energy out of me, as opposed to being in the garden, where

I always feel filled up, where the garden energies actually seem to dance through me.

John died in 1995. At the end he was very ill, but he continued writing and taping thoughts for his last publication, *Making a Good End*. Sometimes, he would come out and sit in the sun and share his ideas about this book or about having to live out deeper and deeper levels of his earlier booklet, *On Living with Diminishment*. Other times we would talk about what he thought needed to be done in the garden and I would be the worker bee. I never felt used by that in any way. There was always so much give and take, so much richness.

At the same time, I felt a need to share a garden more intensely and on a more regular basis. And at just that moment, one of my best friends asked me if I would like to garden with her. Carolyn and I liked to do outdoor things together, but she had never been interested in gardening. Now, her first child was leaving home for college and suddenly, she said, she had a tremendous urge to plant a garden. But her yard was shaded, too. We put an ad in the paper, asking for a sunny garden spot in exchange for half of our crop and within days we got a response from a man who needed help keeping up with his plot in a community garden. Another miracle! He no longer gardens, but Carolyn and I have been part of this beautiful urban half-acre, along with 19 others, for 12 years now.

This garden is different from any of my other gardens because it is not all vegetables. Carolyn loves flowers, so half the garden is planted with flowers. She laughs at me because I still refer to it as the "vegetable garden." But the productivity of growing vegetables is deeply ingrained in me. My father was a highly energetic, highly successful man. He made one stab at growing a garden. Vegetables, of course. To grow corn, he built up mounds of earth and put a fish head in with each seed. The corn stalks grew eight feet tall, but the night before he went out to harvest his perfect crop, the raccoons ate every last ear of corn. That was the end for him. If the garden wasn't productive, Dad wasn't going to waste his time on it!

I had been very successful growing vegetables and the only flowers I had planted until this garden had been around the edges to keep the pests out. It was a challenge for me to turn potentially productive garden space over to beauty. Now I love the flowers as much as Carolyn and last winter we spent a whole afternoon drinking tea at the kitchen table and going through catalogs to find new flowers to try. Some of those were bells of Ireland, giant alium, and obedient plant, which we learned got its name because it bends so willingly into different shapes for arranging.

This garden is different from the others, too, because I'm a different person. It is the garden of my 50s, a decade of reflection and weaving together the threads of my life. What do we talk about now as we turn the soil and plant seeds and pull weeds? Children graduating, marrying, making their way in the world. Parents aging, ill, dying. Our own aches and pains. What we are doing. What our deepest desires are for the time we have left, now that we understand that our lives here on earth are finite.

Staying close to the earth and learning from the rhythms of the seasons feels more important than ever. There are so many metaphors for life in a garden and while I have always been aware of them, they seem to hold more meaning for me now that I am older. For example, for plants to grow well, you have to be willing to thin them and give them adequate space. There are also times when I have to thin out my life. Thinning the carrots reminds me of this, hard as it is to yank out those pretty little lacy green tassels. I must get rid of the "shoulds" and "if onlys" that live inside of me, and from time to time I must let go of certain responsibilities and activities that no longer serve me in order to allow new things to enter my life and grow.

Turning the soil is also a powerful metaphor for me. As I dig in, lift, and turn, there is a corresponding lightening or opening inside. What is added includes sunshine, oxygen, space, and sometimes humus or manure. In the garden I am opened up, exposed for awhile, and usually the additions are beneficial, encouraging me to "lighten up" and let go of the tightness with which I habitually hold my life together.

When I share the digging and turning with a friend, we are both opened up by the process, able to hear each other at a deeper level. We can reflect from a common ground of experience, yet hear each other's uniqueness and allow each enough space to grow. Turning the soil gives seeds fertile ground in which to grow and allows the right time in darkness, where darkness is rest and regeneration, where darkness is not a foe. We are given time to be with new thoughts and ideas, space to experience new ways of being without the direct sunlight or criticism that causes premature withering. Secrets are safe in the garden, gently contained without judgement.

Taking the time to really see the wonder and beauty of this world is another lesson my garden has taught me. Have you ever seen a baby cucumber just beginning to emerge from the back end of the cucumber flower? The flower is a beautiful little yellow bloom and then right off the back of it is this tiny, tiny cucumber. When I first noticed it years ago, I thought it was amazing. I still think it is one of the most beautiful things in the world, and I grow cucumbers every year just to see it. With a garden partner, I get to share the delight, to show off the wonder of a baby cucumber or a first carrot with the rapture of a proud mama.

And, of course, it requires patience to grow a garden. I've done a lot of quilting and people often say to me, "You must have so much patience to be able to do that." I laugh, because I don't see that in myself. Yet it's true. The beauty of a quilt reveals itself tiny piece by tiny piece, and you have to have patience to see it through. I have patience when I know that loving care is going to create something beautiful, like a quilt, something that will give warmth and beauty. I have that same kind of patience for cultivating a garden, especially when at the same time I am cultivating a friendship. Both of them, a garden and a friendship, grow slowly, day by day, piece by piece. Both create a sense of being connected to something that is lovely. Both have the potential to bring beauty and joy into my life. Gardening with a friend multiplies the pleasure of something I already love.

Garden Tips

Each of the women featured in this book has offered some of her favorite gardening tips. For more tips and to view photographs of the women, visit www.gardenvoices.com.

SUSAN'S GARDEN TIPS

1. Choose flowers that you love and worry later about what fits. You can always move a plant, and if it dies, you can learn from the experience.
2. If you are making a path, put down a weed barrier and sand before laying the stones so that you don't have to hand clip so often.
3. Don't let your garden add more guilt to you life. Give yourself permission to work in it only when you feel like being in your garden.
4. Have a mammogram every year.

SUE'S GARDEN TIPS

1. Prune your garden as necessary. For me, removing dead branches and leaves is a metaphor for letting go of and trimming away what has died in my life.
2. I use Miracle Grow in my garden—my plants love it and I love the name!
3. Use at least two inches of mulch on your flower beds to keep the soil moist and stop the weeds from growing. I think of it as putting a lovely blanket on my beds.

Joan's Garden Tips

Because I sell my produce at farmer's markets, I want to pick my crops when they will be most flavorful and at their best. There's a best time to pick almost everything.

1. Pick lettuce the same day you eat it.
2. To have blueberries at the peak of flavor, pick them after the sun is off of them—in the evening or night, but before any dew settles.
3. Pick parsley and cilantro in the morning.
4. Pick basil in the evening, about 8 o'clock.
5. Thyme and other woodier plants, like oregano and rosemary, can be picked at any time. So can peas and beans.
6. Pick tomatoes at any time except when they're wet. That's mainly to prevent disease from spreading.

Nancy's Garden Tips

1. Use pine needles to make a path between flower beds.
2. Garden with a partner when possible. It is fun and it doubles creativity.
3. Use the natural flow and shape of the land to design your pathways and garden.

Michiko's Garden Tips

1. Plant things that are beautiful and intriguing and that reward you for your hard work.
2. Water your garden in the morning.
3. Don't fertilize your tomatoes after you plant them.

Carol's Garden Tips

1. When deer eat your prize geraniums (and everything else), plant silk flowers among the live greens.
2. Remember: Gardening and painting are one percent talent and 99 percent perspiration. Every famous artist was once a beginner.
3. If you have petunia worms, fill two glasses with wine and creep up on them with a flashlight after dark. Push the pests into one glass of wine and toast the evening and yourself with the other glass!
4. Be grateful for every day and all the beauty in it.

Eleanor's Garden Tips

1. Invite people into your garden. It's a great way to share your joy and make new friends.
2. If you put a fence around your garden, leave an inch or two between the boards so that when it gets hot, the garden will have some ventilation.
3. Don't take too much advice from others about your garden. Experiment, have fun, and see what you can discover on your own.
4. Keep a garden journal. Then when you're in your eighties, you can read it and enjoy your garden all over again.

Francie's Garden Tips

Plant remedies and hints from my mother (and, undoubtedly, countless other Italian mothers before her):

1. Gargle with an infusion of sage for a sore throat.
2. Chew parsley to cleanse the breath.
3. Lay lavender flowers and foliage in woolen clothes to drive away moths.
4. Sprinkle chopped garlic around fruit trees to keep worms from eating the fruit.
5. Plant parsley on Good Friday; according to folklore, it has to go to hell and back seven times before it sprouts (parsley is notoriously slow in sprouting).

Beth's Garden Tips

1. Be attentive in your garden to the sacredness of the life forms.
2. Appreciate and care for them as part of yourself.
3. Marvel in the uniqueness and beauty of each flower, tree, and shrub, and celebrate their essence.
4. Be in the moment, mindful of the soil, the sunlight, the gentle breezes, the birds and other creatures as you work and commune.
5. Be gentle and forgiving of yourself when you are not in tune with or are neglectful of your garden. Each moment is a new beginning.

JULIE'S AND ZOE'S GARDEN TIPS

1. Take very good care of your soil. Each fall, dig in nutrients like cow manure and compost. Use leaf mulch if you can because it decomposes more slowly and is better than hardware store compost for building healthy soil.

2. Don't weed your garden when the ground is wet because your shoes will pick up mud and track weed seeds through your garden.

3. Choose some "old reliables" for your garden that will grow for sure. Day lily bulbs, for example, can be planted upside down and they'll *still* grow for you.

4. Do yoga so your back doesn't ache when you weed.

5. Sleep in your garden once in a while.

MARY'S GARDEN TIPS

1. Take time to savor the inconspicuous, the invisible, the unexpected—for instance, the flash of iridescent turquoise from a tiny beetle, the delicate scent of spicebush flowers and the pungency of tomato leaves, the twig that turns out to be a praying mantis, the patterns of spore cases on the underside of fern fronds. A hand lens in a valuable garden tool.

2. Be acutely aware of water as an increasingly scarce resource. Choose plants that, once established, rarely need more water than rain brings; group plants that are likely to need extra (saving work as well as water); grade and plant so that rainwater soaks into the ground instead of running off.

3. Make your garden a good neighbor to the gardens and gardeners around you, and especially to nearby natural areas, parks, and roadsides. Invasive, hard-to-control alien plants, a nuisance in gardens, are a serious threat to the native plants of our dwindling natural habitats.

JUDY'S GARDEN TIPS

1. If at all possible, do not water plants by hand-holding a hose. It is very hard to get enough water deep enough into root systems to do any good. Use a sprinkler, or even better, a drip hose with a timer.
2. Remember that good soil is the most important ingredient in growing things well. Garden soil needs to be a mixture that holds water and that allows oxygen to get to the roots.
3. Do not mulch iris or blue lobelia or cardinal flower. They like their bases exposed. Iris need almost full sun and should be lifted and divided, checking for borers, every three to five years.

If you would like to know more about the women in
Garden Voices, visit

www.gardenvoices.com

Photos of the women and their gardens
Their garden tips and favorite books
Excerpts from their stories
Reading group guide questions